D1083108

Strategic Communications for Nonprofit Organizations

SEVEN STEPS TO CREATING A SUCCESSFUL PLAN

Second Edition

Sally J. Patterson
Janel M. Radtke

John Wiley & Sons, Inc.

Dedicated to my grandson
Benjamin Sandoval
who taught me the wonder of magic minutes.

For general information on our other products and services, or technical support, please contact our Customer Care Department within the United States at 800-762-2974, outside the United States at 317-572-3993, or fax 317-572-4002.

Wiley also publishes its books in a variety of electronic formats. Some content that appears in print may not be available in electronic books.

For more information about Wiley products, visit our web site at http://*www.wiley.com*.

Library of Congress Cataloging-in-Publication Data:

ISBN-13: 978-0-470-40122-4

10 9 8 7 6 5 4 3 2 1

Acknowledgments

In 1993, Janel Radtke inspired me with her vision of a program designed to help nonprofit executives think more strategically about using communications to advance their mission. I became an advocate and a collaborator as she sought to interest others in making this dream come true. With support from Frank Karel, Joan Hollendonner and Vicki Weisfeld of the Robert Wood Johnson Foundation, an interdisciplinary team was convened to answer the question, "What should every nonprofit executive know about communications in order to leverage his or her work?" A theoretical framework was designed, a workshop model was crafted, and templates for a strategic communication plan were created. Janel, Tamar Abrams and I took the model on the road and worked with RWJF grantees and others to test and refine that model.

This book is built on the core principles of the Radiant Communications model—mission driven, audience focused, and action oriented.

In the 10 years since Janel's death, our model has evolved, and the training team has grown. I would like to thank Tamar Abrams, Linda Cummings, Sam Davis, John Fairbanks, Buddy Gill, and Steve Otto for the many memorable moments we shared. We brainstormed, collaborated, and challenged each other to ensure that we gave our clients the very best communications tools and expertise. Priscilla Cavalca and Todd Nedwick managed the workshops and follow-up and allowed the team to focus on our work and the needs of the participants.

Books are written in isolation but become manuscripts, page proofs, and, ultimately, books with the help of talented editors. My thanks to Susan McDermott, Senior Editor, and Natasha Andrews-Noel and Lisa Vuoncino, Production Editors, of John Wiley & Sons, for their guidance, support, and advice throughout this process.

Since those early days, hundreds of nonprofits have followed the Radiant model and risen to our challenge to create bold and integrated communications strategies. This book is dedicated to them and the thousands of individuals who work at nonprofit organizations trying to make our world a better place. You are my inspiration.

Contents

About the Authors

Sally J. Patterson is the president of Radiant Communications, a strategic communications firm that counsels nonprofit leaders on organizational issues including board development, communications planning, executive coaching, and leadership transitions. Based in Washington DC, she has more than 25 years of strategic communications and public policy expertise including 10 years with public opinion research firms. She has provided strategic communications consultation and training to more than 700 nonprofit organizations.

Radiant Communications is a team of innovative professionals who challenge organizations to create bold and integrated communications strategies. Our approach is marked by a commitment to provide clients with the analytical and management expertise necessary to achieve their mission and advocacy goals. For more information, see our Web site at www.radiantstrategies.com.

Janel M. Radtke was the founder and first president of Radiant Communications, Inc. In this role, Janel worked with nonprofit organizations assisting them in the planning, creation, implementation, and evaluation of their communications. Prior to launching Radiant Communications, Ms. Radtke was the first executive director of the Center for Strategic Communications, where she educated nonprofits about the creation and utilization of a strong and dynamic communications environment. Before joining the Center, Ms. Radtke was vice president for communications at Planned Parenthood Federation of America and co-founded the New York Law School's Communications Media Center. Ms. Radtke died in 1999.

Preface

Strategic Communications as a Way to Effect Social Change

Communications is about building understanding. It is about nurturing change. When a national tragedy, like the bombing of the World Trade Center or Hurricane Katrina, occurs and we watch television coverage or read news accounts but also discuss the matter with friends and colleagues, we are changed. When an issue is discussed and decided by the local school board, we are changed. When we attend a rally, read a book, participate in a conference, we are changed. Social change, political change, community change . . . *change* is the business of the nonprofit community.

Strategic communications is the key to successful social change. It is mission driven, audience focused, and action oriented. It is the art of expressing ideas combined with the science of transmitting information. It is crafting the message so that it motivates target audiences to act in a desired manner. It integrates all aspects of the nonprofit organization—public education, programs and services, advocacy, membership, and fund-raising—into a single cohesive and potentially powerful mechanism. It helps to project a positive image of the organization, focuses public attention, strengthens community partnerships, and maximizes scarce organizational resources to achieve social change.

Today's communications environment is fast-paced, chaotic, and complex. Many people feel overwhelmed by the mix of media, the bombardment of messages, and the intensity of the emotions, promotions, and proclamations from advertisers, media mavens, and commercial and for-profit interests. Nonprofit organizations face an immense challenge in trying to attract attention for their missions and their messages.

There is no general public anymore, only target audiences, key constituencies, and influentials who, by virtue of their education, income, and activism, have a more powerful impact on community affairs and public policy than their numbers would suggest. New electronic, wireless, and online communications options have presented us with dozens of new strategies to consider, thereby making the communications process more challenging.

Strategic communications plans are organic documents. They are frameworks that drive the work of the organization. They are active staff directives, and they do not belong on a shelf. Circumstances surrounding the nonprofit organization's communications change almost daily, and so should the communications plan. The plan is a reminder to the organization, its staff, and its board to routinely challenge itself:

- What are we trying to achieve?
- Whom are we trying to reach?
- What do we want them to do?
- How do we encourage them to do it?
- How will we know if we have succeeded?

By maximizing resources, focusing on potentially supportive audiences, and conveying the value, services, and impact of the organization—by being strategic about communications—the nonprofit can achieve positive social change, fulfilling its mission, advancing its programs and policies, and making its value known.

Getting the Most Out of This Book

*S*trategic Communications for Nonprofit Organizations: Seven Steps to Creating a Successful Plan offers a conceptual framework and a step-by-step process for developing a strategic communications plan for the nonprofit organization. It is based on the core principles and approach developed by Radiant Communications, Inc., and our training teams, in partnership with hundreds of nonprofit clients.

Intended Audiences

This workbook is written to help nonprofit boards and staff to develop effective communications strategies and work plans. For seasoned communications professionals, it offers a useful refresher on communications principles and a source book of fundamental concepts and techniques. For those without experience, it offers an introduction to strategic communications planning, tools for addressing communications challenges, and a template for developing a strategic communications plan to achieve the goals of the organization.

This book is also directed to grant makers in an effort to help them understand how integral communications is to the success of the programs they fund. When a grantee practices strategic communications, a foundation's investment is leveraged because the impact of that grant is greater than it would have been without the communications component. Nonprofit organizations are in the communications business—and that means their work is not only about *what happened* but also about *what is happening, what the organization wants to happen, and why.* Communications efforts cannot occur after the fact; they must be ongoing and woven into the fabric of the programs to which the organization and the foundation are committed.

Strategic Communications Plan Framework

The strategic communications plan is an implementation strategy to help the organization achieve its programmatic goals. It is a companion to the organization's strategic plan and builds on the mission, vision, program goals and objectives, and business plan of the organization. The communications planning process sets measurable goals for reaching, informing, and motivating the audiences that are essential to the organization's mission.

The seven steps to the strategic communications planning process are:

Step One: Preparing to Plan: Essential Building Blocks. Effective strategic communications plans depend on an organization's willingness to ask the tough questions, to consider the possibilities of bold actions, to be disciplined about the allocation of resources, to be diligent in the pursuit of community partnerships and donor support, and to be persistent in the implementation, monitoring, and evaluation of the plan. Before engaging in strategic communications planning, the nonprofit organization should set clear goals for the planning process; should determine roles and responsibilities for the chief executive officer, senior staff, and board; and should decide whether outside allies should also be included in the process. The formation of a communications action team (CAT) will facilitate the planning process and ensure that the planning does not get bogged down.

Step Two: Foundation of the Plan: The Situation Analysis. The strategic communications plan supports the work of the organization. It must reflect the mission, goals, objectives, and strategies that the organization has established for fulfilling its vision. For that reason, the strategic plan needs to reflect the environment surrounding the organization, including an analysis of the internal and external forces affecting the organization. The internal analysis examines the organization's operations and identifies its strengths and weaknesses. The external analysis examines the outside forces that influence every organization and seeks to identify immediate opportunities and threats.

Step Three: Focusing the Plan: Target Audiences. Successful communications plans put the information needs and preferences of the audience first. This step asks the question "Whom do we need to succeed?" Nonprofit organizations need to focus their communications efforts and resources on those who are already engaged in work that matches the organization's mission, those who already care about the issue, and those who can be easily prepared to become involved in the issue.

Step Four: Fostering Audience Support: Communications Objectives. Communications objectives define what is expected of each target audience and speaks to the question "What do we want them to do?" Successful communications objectives are SMART: Specific, Measurable, Appropriate, Realistic, and Time-bound. Without these five elements, communications objectives are only wishes and the strategic plan is but a dream of what could be.

Step Five: Promoting the Nonprofit Organization: Issue Frames and Message Development. Message development is the component of strategic communications planning that ensures that the target audiences are motivated to take the actions that will support the organization's mission. Effective, persuasive messages must inform, motivate and involve audiences. Messages must be mission driven, audience focused, and action oriented.

Step Six: Advancing the Plan: Vehicles and Dissemination Strategies. An effective communications plan relies on coordinated dissemination strategies that utilize all five forms of communication: face-to-face, print, audio, video, and electronic communications. The plan must reinforce the mission, values, and messages in several different formats for maximum impact on each target audience.

Step Seven: Ensuring that the Plan Succeeds: Measurement and Evaluation. Knowing the success measures for the communications plan ensures that staff, board, volunteers, and others remain focused on what needs to be done and why. Clear impact measures, established at the beginning of the planning process, make it easier to ascertain what is working, what needs to be changed, and what can safely be abandoned.

After these steps have been completed, the worksheets are transferred into a written plan that includes:

- An executive summary or overview of the plan
- The organization's mission and value statements
- The communications objectives
- Clear communications strategies and dissemination plans for each priority audience
- Key messages
- Main products and services to be developed
- A budget
- An implementation plan (with timeline)
- Clear benchmarks for evaluating success

Structure of the Workbook

The workbook is organized to follow the flow of the strategic communications process. Each chapter outlines the basic principles and approach necessary to complete the step. Within each chapter are *guiding questions* to allow the organization to quickly assess its needs and objectives for each step in the process, followed by comprehensive worksheets to provide the building blocks for the strategic communications plan. Blank worksheets are included at the end of each chapter as well as on the dedicated Web site associated with this book (www.wiley.com/go/nonprofitcommunications2).

In addition, each chapter includes *Checklists* and *Rules of the Road* to help direct the CAT through each step. Case examples and a template for the strategic communications plan are also provided to illustrate various components of the communications plan and to demonstrate how it all pulls together into a working plan of action.

How to Use This Workbook

This book is a helpful overview of the strategic communications planning process. The reader should review it in its entirety to understand the core concepts and the relationship between each of the steps toward building the comprehensive plan. At many points in the process, the desired outcome might suggest alternative courses of actions. In order to make the best choices, being familiar with the flow of the strategic communications process is invaluable.

Nevertheless, there are also circumstances in which an organization is focused on a particular challenge or problem, such as the need to respond quickly to a communications challenge or crisis. When resources are limited, when time is short, or when the organization is facing an immediate and particular problem, this workbook can also guide the reader through a targeted response. Specifically, the book contains methods for establishing a crisis response strategy for emergencies and controversies and a communications audit for helping an organization pinpoint specific challenges that may benefit from a more tailored response. In those circumstances, the guiding questions and targeted use of the worksheets may serve the needs of the organization well.

Throughout the book, it is assumed that the work will be done by a communications action team. More hands and minds will strengthen the process and ensure that the strategic communications plan is competed and implemented by the entire organization. However, there are times when the burden for this type of planning falls to a single individual. In these cases, as you complete the worksheets and the plan, test your hypotheses from the perspective of others in the organization: board, stakeholders, staff, volunteers, and clients.

Whether the workbook is used in its entirety or only to focus on a particular challenge, the principles and tools provided are designed to improve the effectiveness of the communications and outreach efforts of the nonprofit organization. When carefully completed and applied, the seven steps are designed to support the nonprofit organization in its efforts to achieve its mission and to promote lasting social change. Applying the practical tools, in whole or in part, will improve the communications practices and advance the work of the nonprofit organization. They are presented to encourage nonprofits to focus on the possibilities.

How to Use the Web Site

The worksheets, Strategic Communications Plan template, and the Planet 3000 case study are also available at a dedicated Web site. It can be found at www.wiley.com/go/nonprofitcommunications2. These templates can be easily downloaded for your individual use, the use of your communications action team (CAT) and to introduce the model to the board, senior management, and other stakeholders.

Readiness for Strategic Communications Planning

Worksheet 1 found at the end of this chapter can help the organization determine its communications needs and focus its planning process. This checklist is designed to help senior management and/or the board determine where to put their energies in addressing the communications needs of the organization. This exercise can be done collectively by senior staff, the executive committee of the board, and/or the entire board. Results of this assessment should be shared broadly to generate interest and build support for the strategic communications planning process.

Worksheet 1   Readiness for Strategic Communications

Key
Y = Yes, in place   NW = Needs more work   N = No, not in place

Y NW N   1. Does our organization have a clear strategic vision that supports our mission and guides our communications work?

Y NW N   2. Is our mission statement a concise, accurate description of what our organization is and the work that we do?

Y NW N   3. Does our organization have a strategic plan that guides the staff in its communications and outreach efforts?

Y NW N   4. If not, do we need to conduct a communications audit?

Y NW N   5. Is our communications and outreach work successfully advancing the mission of our organization?

Y NW N   6. Do we know who the priority audiences are? Do we know what we want them to do?

Y NW N   7. Are our messages clear, concise and designed to motivate our priority audiences to take action?

Y NW N   8. Do the strategies and communications vehicles that we use work in concert to achieve the maximum communications impact?

Y NW N   9. Do we have a clear mechanism for monitoring and evaluating our communications work?

Y NW N   10. Are our internal communications structures and strategies effective across the organization?

Y NW N   11. Have we allocated sufficient resources to ensure the success of our strategic communications plan?

Priorities for the Strategic Communications Plan

CHAPTER 2

Strategic Communications Planning Process

The term *strategic communications* describes the combination of plans, goals, practices, and tools with which a nonprofit organization sends consistent messages about its mission, values, and accomplishments. Under the strategic communications domain are a variety of activities that occur, to some degree, in most nonprofit organizations, including public education, advocacy, membership, programs and services, and fundraising. Depending on the organization's needs, strategic communications may also address issues such as branding the nonprofit, framing issues, and preparing for communication controversies and emergencies (crisis communications). Internal communications—within the board, within the staff, and between board and staff—are also an essential part of the process.

Communications is *strategic* when it is integrated, orchestrated, and ongoing. Frank Karel, founder of the Communications Network, describes it as "a process guided by the relentless pursuit of answers to deceptively simple questions: What do you want to accomplish? Who has to think or act differently for that to happen? What would prompt them to do it?"[1]

Strategic communications persuades, moves, and convinces priority audiences and constituents to help an organization achieve its mission. How the organization articulates its mission, vision, values, and desired outcomes determines whom it draws as supporters, donors, volunteers, and community partners. How it presents itself to its constituencies, the public, opinion leaders, and others determines whether it can leverage resources to achieve the organization's mission. How it defines its issues and policies determines whether the public will become engaged and take appropriate actions.

---

[1]Communications Network, www.commnetwork.org.

Why Strategic Communications Matters

Nonprofit organizations play a significant role in addressing community needs. Through effective community engagement, partnering with organizations that share the same agenda, and advocating before policy makers, nonprofit organizations ensure that the public attention is focused on the needs of the community. The strategic communications plan is an implementation strategy that helps the organization achieve its strategic goals. It is a companion to the overall strategic planning process that builds on the mission and vision statements. Communications planning establishes clear goals and objectives linked to specific programs and services.

It is important to remember that strategic communications is not about marketing, sound bites, spin, or campaign promises, nor is it about fancy brochures, glossy annual reports, and animated Web sites. Despite attempts by well-meaning board members and some public relations consultants to encourage the adoption of commercial marketing practices, the communications needs and challenges of nonprofit organizations are not well served by this approach. Advertising, marketing, and public relations are designed to help the for-profit sector expand market share and increase company revenues. Nonprofit organizations strive to maintain revenues and income streams as well, but the communications strategy of a nonprofit organization must be focused on advancing its mission and increasing the community base of support for its work. The challenge for nonprofits is to articulate their values clearly so that people can relate to the mission, connect to the underlying values, and commit to take action to support the organization.

An organization that takes a strategic approach to communications uses language that is simple, clear, and direct and crafts messages that are action-oriented. It targets its resources effectively to build public understanding, confidence, and loyalty. It must build public trust and individual commitment to its priorities. In extraordinary circumstances, it is public confidence that will help the nonprofit weather the crisis of the day or the unexpected bend in the road.

Benefits of Strategic Communications Planning

Strategic communications provides a framework that helps ensure that every staff and board member is working from the same set of assumptions and understands how their work fits into the broader work of the organization. A strategic framework can

- *Help in setting priorities and clarifying future direction.* As strategic communications becomes integrated, staff members will approach their work in a new way, routinely asking "Whom are we trying to reach, what do we want them to do, and how will we know if we have succeeded?'' Board members will have a framework for assessing the progress of the organization and for determining how they can integrate their efforts into the organization's work.

- *Improve performance and stimulate creative thinking.* When everyone on the staff and board understands why certain audiences are important and what actions the organization wants from those audiences, it is easier to focus planning and creativity on common objectives.

- *Build teamwork and expertise.* When an organization highlights the synergy of communications activity with all aspects of its work, communications staff, program staff, and development staff begin to collaborate and share information in new ways. They look for ways to set priorities, coordinate resource allocation, and improve internal communications.

- *Use limited resources effectively.* By setting clear, consistent messages and determining priority audiences and dissemination strategies in advance of launching projects, staff members can maximize the opportunity to combine messages and to use certain communications vehicles with multiple audiences. Considering the value of the investment against desired impact may encourage an organization to issue a straightforward annual financial report instead of spending scarce communications resources on a glossy annual report. Instead of a set of brochures targeting volunteers, prospective donors, community supporters, and others who might care about its work, an organization may be able to weave all of those opportunities, messages, and themes into a single brochure.

Roles and Responsibilities in Strategic Communications Planning

The staff, with leadership from the chief executive, has primary responsibility for developing and implementing the strategic communications plan. The board inspires and guides communications planning and is involved in certain aspects of its implementation. The board is also responsible for monitoring the impact and success of the strategic communications plan to ensure that it supports the overall mission and strategic direction of the organization. Exhibit 2.1 outlines the different roles and responsibilities for board and staff throughout each of the steps of the strategic communications planning process.

To ensure that the strategic communications planning process stays on track and is not overtaken by other, more immediate organizational priorities, it is important to create a command team to take leadership of the

Exhibit 2.1   Strategic Communications Planning: Board versus Staff Roles

Task	Board Role	Staff Role
Review of Mission and Goals	Every 3 years, board reviews staff recommendations for new goals and program objectives.	Staff members develop recommended goals and program objectives for the board to review and ratify.
Situation Analysis	Review the analysis prepared by staff. Supplement with its own perspectives on the needs and trends influencing the work of the organization.	Compile data that examines the political, economic, social, demographic, and technological factors that affect the organization.
Audience Identification	Identify key audiences to be included in the strategic communications plan.	Identify key audiences to be targeted through the organization's activities.
Message Development	Support staff in developing tailored messages to meet the information needs of the targeted audiences.	Develop and propose messages to be used with priority audiences; work with the board to ensure that the messages will be effective.
Plan for Communications Vehicles	Monitor and evaluate the quality and effectiveness of the communications vehicles. Use the materials in its outreach on behalf of the organization. Provide feedback on the effectiveness of the materials.	Develop a production plan for the development of communications vehicles, including the design elements to support the goals of the communications plan.
Timeline and Budget	Ensure adequate resources to fulfill the plan.	Prepare the program plan and budget. Set realistic time frames for action.
Monitoring and Evaluation	Review the reports prepared by the staff; evaluate own performance in supporting the plan. Look for additional ways to support the work of the staff.	Prepare routine reports for the board's review; make recommendations for modifying the strategic plan based on results and newly emerging needs.

SOURCE: Sally Patterson, *Generating Buzz: Strategic Communications for Nonprofit Boards* (Washington, DC: BoardSource, 2006), p. 60.

communications planning process. Three alternative planning teams are possible, depending on the scope of the communications needs of the nonprofit organization:

1. A communications action team (CAT) if the organization is prepared to launch the strategic communications planning process
2. A communications audit team if a review of the current state of the communications work is all that is desired
3. A crisis communications control team, if the organization is preparing a contingency plan for responding to crises and controversies

Communications Action Team

To ensure that the strategic communications planning process moves forward in a systematic way, it is important to designate a staff team with responsibility for creating the process, monitoring progress, engaging broad participation, and ensuring momentum. One way to secure the necessary involvement to support the strategic communications plan is to create a communications action team (CAT) charged with all facets of the organization's communications effort.

All too often the individuals within the organization who are most enthusiastic about pursuing a strategic communications plan fail to reach out for help; or if they do, they ask staff members who have the most on their plates and are hard-pressed to take on yet another commitment. Creating a CAT expands participation, provides multiple perspectives, and grounds the plan in the fiber of the organization's work.

Because a communications plan is a "living" thing—it is not something to be completed one week and put away until next month—it will require continued effort on the part of those most directly involved. Even if it is a single phone call or listserve posting, some action should occur with the plan every day.

What the CAT Does.   The CAT is in charge of doing the research—or working with outside experts to have it done—to create the communications plan. It is responsible for building the plan and securing buy-in from other constituencies within the organization. The CAT also implements the plan—supervises others who may be responsible for performing individual tasks that comprise the various strategies—and evaluates the effectiveness of the communications effort regularly to fine-tune and update the plan as needed.

The CAT should meet regularly (preferably once a week, but no less than once a month) during the development of the plan, via conference calls or face to face. At these meetings, team members should review and evaluate the different parts of the plan, not only to update each other on how the plan is unfolding but also to change direction when necessary.

Determine the Criteria for the CAT.   There are four characteristics to consider when recruiting CAT members:

1. Expertise or skills
2. Attitude toward the organization's communications effort

3. Character or personality traits
4. Current responsibilities within the organization

Different organizations—as well as the individuals leading the charge and advocating creation of a communications plan—will have different wish lists when it comes to the composition of the CAT. That is why it is useful to brainstorm with others inside the organization to determine who might best fit into the team and be willing and able to do the work. Make a list of the critical variables to determine what features are important for a successful CAT for the organization and for the challenges that it currently faces.

Although certain types of expertise or skills are essential for the team, other qualities may be just as important to the team's success. For example, an excellent writer who does not easily share his or her ideas with others may not be a good CAT member.

In addition, it is important to recruit individuals from different departments or areas of the organization to ensure that all program goals and operational realities are being addressed within the communications plan, including internal communications, production schedules, budgetary considerations, and others. It may also be valuable to have a board member or a well-informed volunteer on the CAT to provide an external perspective on behalf of stakeholders.

Desired Qualities for CAT Members. The chart below lists characteristics that have proven to be important for potential CAT members. The leader for the strategic planning process, in consultation with the chief executive, should determine which characteristics will be most valuable to the process.

Expertise/Skills	Attitude	Character	Department/Program
Interpersonal skills	Enthusiastic	Team player	Communications
Writing	Good listener	Committed	Development
Public relations	Meets deadlines	Creative	Public affairs
Technology	Passionate	Leader	Administrative/Information management
Graphic design	Positive, "can-do"	Honest	Training
Connections	Aware of the power of language, images, symbols	Self-motivated	Volunteer services

Identify Potential Members for the CAT. Once the essential skills and expertise have been determined, it is important to consider the people within the organization who possess the right knowledge or expertise—or others who might be interested in volunteering their time to the effort. For example, someone who has been with the organization for a long time may know all of its communications assets but, just as readily, may be the one who says "We've tried that before and it didn't work." Who possesses the critical traits, skills, and expertise? It is important to identify potential candidates with the right mix of skills and character for the CAT and to invite them to join the project. If possible, when recruiting the members of the CAT, explain why they have been selected, what it is hoped they will contribute to the CAT, and the length and amount of time the strategic communications planning process is likely to take. If necessary, ask the person's supervisor beforehand if it is possible to include this person in the CAT.

The CAT should consist of at least three people. The more people a team has, the stronger pool of resources it has for moving the plan. With more people, there is also a greater need for coordinating logistics and calendars. If your CAT is large (more than seven people), it might be necessary to break the team into working groups that mix and match people according to strategies or objectives.

Recruit Members of the CAT. Once the individuals have been selected based on the criteria identified as important for team members, use these questions to ensure that each member is able to meet the demands of the strategic communications planning process.

- Can the person commit sufficient time and attention for at least six months?
- Is the person comfortable as a team player?
- Can the person take charge of a task and get it done without supervision?
- Does the person usually meet deadlines?
- Is the person interested in learning more about communications tools, techniques, and strategies?

Worksheet 2, found at the end of this chapter, can be used to help form a communications action team (CAT).

Rules of the Road: Creating a Communications Action Team

1. The chief executive and the leader of the strategic communications planning process should review the suggested criteria listed above and determine the desired criteria for the CAT. Together, they should consider the departments and programs that should be represented and identify potential individuals for the CAT, being sure to factor in attitude and character considerations.

2. Recruit the members for the CAT, making sure that each recruit understands the time commitment and the expectations involved.

Communications Audit Team

As a first step in the strategic planning process, the CAT may determine that a communications audit is necessary. A communications audit is a comprehensive analysis of an organization's communications—internal and/or external—to review communications needs, policies, practices, and capacity in order to improve organization efficiency and effectiveness. The CAT may conduct the communications audit or determine that a separate communications audit team should be formed.

What the Audit Team Does.   The communications audit team conducts interviews with top management and key internal stakeholders to determine their attitudes and beliefs about communication and to pinpoint communications problems. It collects collateral communications materials, conducts an inventory, and prepares an analysis of the communications products developed by the organization. This analysis includes all existing communications materials, communications vehicles, and programs: media kits, letterhead, fact sheets, brochures, publications, audiovisuals, Web material, and any other materials used by the organization. The team identifies communications issues that must be addressed by the organization in four key areas:

1. Management and production
2. Messaging and branding
3. Identification of efficient and effective communications tools
4. Techniques and issues to be addressed throughout the strategic communications planning process

The communications audit team also meets with the CAT to present findings and to inform the strategic communications planning process.

Whom to Recruit.   Members of the communications audit team also can be the members of the CAT as long as they have these skills and expertise: operations (human relations, policy, editorial, and production), marketing and membership/outreach, and communications.

Expertise/Skills	Attitude	Character	Department/Program
Strategic thinker	Enthusiastic	Team player	Communications
Writing	Good listener	Committed	Development
Public relations	Meets deadlines	Creative	Public affairs
Technology	Passionate		Administration
Graphic design	Positive, "can-do"		Technology
Operations	Aware of the power of language, images, symbols		Production
Organization-wide perspective			

Rules of the Road: Communications Audit Team

1. The CAT determines the criteria for the communications audit team and determines whether the CAT will perform the communications audit or if different individuals and/or different talents are necessary to complete this work. It should also consider the departments and programs that should be represented, including human resources, membership, marketing, and communications.
2. If research is to be done in-house, the CAT ensures that the team has a member with good facilitation and group process skills.
3. The CAT recruits someone to oversee the inventory of communications vehicles. This must be a person who is knowledgeable about the organization's branding platform and the elements of graphic design.

Worksheet 3, found at the end of this chapter, can be used to help form a communications audit team.

Crisis Communications Planning

Conducting a comprehensive strategic communications planning process may provide the ideal opportunity for the organization to consider whether it is prepared in the event of a crisis or a controversy. Nonprofit organizations, depending on their missions, generally deal with two types of crises: emergencies and controversies. *Emergencies* are predictable events that cause havoc for an organization or the people it serves and that may harm its ability to perform its mission. There are five major types of emergencies:

1. Physical or psychological injury to people
2. The inability to continue important organizational operations
3. Damage to or destruction of facilities
4. Financial loss
5. Spillover effects from something that has affected other people or other organizations

The responsibility for handling emergencies rests primarily with the staff, guided by disaster and risk management plans, with board members providing collateral support where appropriate.

Controversies are crises that threaten the organization's reputation. Fraud accusations, legal disputes, or leadership conflicts are examples of controversies that challenge an organization's integrity and effectiveness. Responding to a controversy usually requires board involvement and, possibly, board leadership.

The crisis communications plan addresses six essential questions:

1. Who is responsible for managing the crisis, and what are his or her duties?
2. Where should the command center be for responding to the crisis?
3. What resources will be needed?
4. Who should be part of the crisis control team, and what are their responsibilities?
5. What information is appropriate to give to the public?
6. Who will speak for the organization?

Crises do not usually get resolved with a single press statement or public announcement. It is important for crisis planners to realize that information needs, target audiences, and messaging will evolve over time, as more facts become known and as events unfold. The best way to deal with a crisis is before it happens. The strategic communications planning process provides an excellent opportunity for the board and staff to develop contingency plans for dealing with crises. A crisis communications planning team made up of both board and staff members should be created. Because crisis situations usually involve board engagement at a higher level that most communications work, both perspectives must be reflected in the planning process.

Crisis Communications Team

The crisis communications planning team is responsible for assessing the possible crises that may confront the organization and for developing the framework for a plan of action in the event of a crisis. Crisis situations require articulate and well-timed communications with all stakeholders and the media. Crisis communications planning is a two-step process. The first step, performed by the crisis communications planning team, is to determine what challenges could affect the organization, what prevention strategies can be implemented, and what materials need to be compiled in advance of a possible crisis. The second step is to form the team that will lead the process when a crisis actually occurs, the crisis control team. Although members of the crisis communications planning team may be members of the crisis control team, decision makers at the top of the organization—the chief executive and the board chair—should provide the leadership when a crisis actually occurs.

 Worksheet 4, found at the end of this chapter, can be used to help form a crisis communications planning team.

Crisis Control Team

When a crisis occurs, a spokesperson (usually the chief executive) is designated to issue public statements, but a crisis control team should be formed to support the spokesperson as the crisis actually unfolds. This team determines the response should an emergency or controversy strike the organization, implements the crisis communications plan, monitors ongoing crisis mitigation, and manages the information flow to the media and all key stakeholders.

When the crisis occurs, the crisis control team must revisit the plan, challenge plan assumptions against what has actually taken place, and determine a course of action, revising roles and responsibilities as necessary. As new information unfolds, the team must assess who needs to know, what additional information is necessary, and what actions need to be taken.

The crisis control team can be board or staff driven, but both board and staff members should be represented. In addition, team members should include a human resources specialist, a financial officer, and a legal authority for the organization. In some circumstances, it may be necessary to recruit grief counselors or other support for those most immediately affected by the crisis. Above all, the team should be comprised of trusted people who can remain focused under pressure.

The chief executive and a board representative should also be members of this team to act as chief spokesperson(s). If someone who was slated to be a member of the crisis control team is involved in the controversy, he or she must be removed from the team. Roles will have to be shifted and the plan altered to meet the changed circumstances.

Expertise/Skills	Attitude	Character	Department/Program
Public relations	Enthusiastic	Team Player	Communications
Quick grasp of difficult situations	Persuasive	Committed	Board of directors
Contingency thinker	Confident	Credible	Public affairs Development
Leader	Positive, ``can-do''	Steadfast	Legal
Has connections with stakeholders	Aware of the power of language, images, symbols	Calm under pressure	Community relations
Public speaker			Finance

Rules of the Road: Crisis Communications Planning Team

1. The CAT determines the criteria for the team. Can the CAT perform the planning functions for the crisis communications plan or are different talents necessary to complete this work?
2. The CAT ensures that the appropriate departments and programs are represented, including human resources, finance, and legal.
3. The chief executive and the board chair determine board participation in the crisis communications planning team and the crisis control team. Board perspective can be particularly helpful in addressing issues related to controversies.
4. The chief executive, board chair, and leader of the CAT factor in attitudes and character considerations such as those suggested for the CAT. In the case of a crisis, it is important to have people who will have a sense of command during intense times, who have the trust of the board and staff, and who will be deemed credible by the media and other external stakeholders.

Take the Time, Make the Time

Once the human resources are committed, setting aside the time to complete the work is the next hurdle in making a communications plan a reality. The importance of making the time to plan, implement, and evaluate the communications effort cannot be stressed enough. Because a communications plan is a living thing—an ongoing process—one task that is delayed or postponed can derail an entire strategy. Thus, finding the time on an individual level becomes more important than allocating sufficient time within the plan itself. For this reason, commitment to the plan by all CAT members is imperative.

Many of the steps of the strategic communications planning process will support the work of the CAT, the audit team and the crisis communications team. The chart that follows (Exhibit 2.2) identifies the worksheets and

Exhibit 2.2   Roadmap for Strategic Communications Planning

	Strategic Communications Planning	Communications Audit	Crisis Communications Planning
1. Readiness for Strategic Communications	XXX	XXX	XXX
2. Form a Communications Action Team	XXX		
3. Form a Communications Audit Team		XXX	
4. Form a Crisis Communications Team			XXX
5. Mission Statement and Goals	XXX	XXX	XXX
6. Communications Audit Summary	XXX	XXX	XXX
7. Situation Analysis	XXX		Optional
8. Strengths, Weaknesses, Opportunities, Threats Worksheet	XXX		Optional
9. SWOT Analysis	XXX		Optional

(Continued)

Exhibit 2.2   (Continued)

	Strategic Communications Planning	Communications Audit	Crisis Communications Planning
10. Community Partners and Stakeholders	XXX		Optional
11. Audience Identification	XXX		
12. Audience Profile	XXX		
13. Develop SMART Communications Objectives	XXX		
14. Simple Framing Analysis	XXX	Optional	
15. Framing Analysis Worksheet	XXX	Optional	
16. Language Worksheet	XXX	Optional	
17. Organization Description	XXX		XXX
18. Develop Persuasive Messages	XXX		XXX
19. Put a Human Face on the Work	XXX		
20. Evaluating Strategic Options	XXX		
21. Evaluate Existing Vehicles and Strategies	XXX		
22. Plan New Vehicles and Strategies	XXX		
23. Putting It All Together	XXX		
24. Develop Outcome Measures	XXX		XXX

action steps that are appropriate for the communications challenge that has been identified and the type of team that has been formed.

No matter how prepared the CAT is, there will be things unanticipated or left undone. Even in these circumstances, a good communications plan ensures that as many pieces as can be put together beforehand are in place, helping what might otherwise be chaos seem only ''terribly busy.'' A strong CAT means that there are people, resources, and processes in place to make the necessary midcourse corrections without creating a crisis for the organization.

Rules of the Road: Tips for Finding the Time

1. The chief executive and the leader of the strategic communication planning process form the appropriate team: communications action team, communications audit team, crisis control team, and/or crisis communications planning team. Define clear roles and responsibilities for each team.

2. The leader of the strategic communications planning process ensures that the CAT does one thing a day, and does it first thing in the morning. It is their responsibility to make the communications tasks a top priority so that, no matter what else happens during the day, the organization's communications efforts remain on track.

3. The CAT must turn their calendars into strategic communications checklists. Each CAT member should mark the dates on their personal calendars for tracking.

4. As the CAT moves forward, it must consider the seamlessness of every strategy, appropriately delegating responsibilities to members of the team. Sometimes it is more efficient to put one person in charge of all the tasks involved with an entire strategy; other times it is better to divide the tasks that comprise a single strategy among several people who work well together and assume responsibility for their department's pieces of the project.

Worksheet 2   Form a Communications Action Team

The communications action team oversees the research, builds the strategic communications plan, ensures buy-in, and implements, monitors, and evaluates the plan.

1. Circle the desired traits needed for the communications action team.

Expertise/Skills	Attitude	Character	Department/Program
Interpersonal skills	Enthusiastic	Team player	Communications
Writing	Good listener	Committed	Development
Public relations	Meets deadlines	Creative	Public affairs
Technology	Passionate	Leadership	Administrative/MIS
Graphic design	Positive, "can-do"	Honest	Training
Connections	Aware of the power of language, images, symbols	Self-motivated	Volunteer services

2. Consider which members of the staff provide the best mix of desired skills, character and attitude for the communications action team.

Name of Individual/ Department	What They Bring to the Team

3. What additional support will we need for the success of the Communications Action Team?

Worksheet 3   Form a Communications Audit Team

The communications audit team conducts stakeholder interviews, evaluates the management of the communications function, conducts the assessment of the content and branding of communications vehicles, and reports to the communications action team.

1. Circle the desired traits needed for the communications audit team.

Expertise/Skills	Attitude	Character	Department/Program
Strategic thinker	Enthusiastic	Team player	Communications
Writing	Good listener	Committed	Development
Public relations	Meets deadlines	Creative	Public affairs
Technology	Passionate		Administration
Graphic design	Positive, "can-do"		Technology
	Aware of the power of language, images, symbols		Production

2. Consider which members of the staff provide the best mix of desired skills, character and attitude for the communications audit team.

Name of Individual/ Department	What They Bring to the Team

3. What additional support will we need for the success of the communications audit team?

Worksheet 4   Form a Crisis Communications Team

The crisis communications team assesses potential crises, develops the framework for a plan of action, evaluates actual crises, and handles the implementation of a crisis response, including the information flow to media and all key stakeholders.

1. Circle the desired traits needed for the crisis communications team.

Expertise/Skills	Attitude	Character	Department/Program
Public relations	Enthusiastic	Team player	Communications
Finance	Persuasive	Committed	Board of directors
Contingency thinker	Confident	Leader	Public affairs
			Development
Legal	Positive, "can-do"	Steadfast	Legal
Has connections with stakeholders	Aware of the power of language, images, symbols	Credible Calm under pressure	Community relations
Public speaker			

2. Consider which members of the staff provide the best mix of desired skills, character, and attitude for the crisis communications team.

Name of Individual/ Department	What they bring to the team
Human Resources	
Legal	
Finance/Operations	
Board Representative	
Official Spokesperson	

3. What additional support will we need for the success of the crisis control team?

Step One: Preparing to Plan Essential Building Blocks

Successful nonprofit organizations engage in strategic planning every three to five years to articulate their vision for the future direction of the organization and to establish goals, objectives, and strategies for fulfilling that vision. A strategic communications plan—with targeted audiences, clear communications objectives, carefully crafted messages, and appropriate strategies and vehicles—supports the implementation of the organization's strategic plan.

Strategic communications builds on the strategic plan and ensures that the organization mobilizes all of its resources to fulfill that plan. It is an important tool to help the organization focus on its mission and meet its goals. Strategic communications is targeted to priority audiences and key stakeholders: persuading, convincing, and moving those audiences to help achieve the organizational mission.

Strategic communications will also help the organization improve performance, stimulate creative thinking, set priorities and clarify future direction, solve major organizational problems, use limited resources more effectively, build teamwork and expertise, and increase its ability to influence the community.

These terms are used in the development of a strategic communications plan:

Mission	**Why** your organization exists
Vision	**Where** your organization wants to be
Goals	**What** your organization wants
Situation analysis	**What** affects your organization
Objectives	**How** your organization makes it happen
Communications objectives	**Who** needs to be reached and why

Strategic Communications Is Grounded in the Mission

A mission statement has to focus on what the institution really tries to do. . . .

The mission is something that transcends today, but (at the same time) guides today and informs today.

—Peter Drucker, *Managing the Non-Profit Organization*

The strategic communications plan must be driven by the underlying values and purposes that define the organization. Every organization has a mission, a purpose, and a reason for being. A mission statement is a written statement using formal language, which is particularly useful in printed pieces, with foundations, donors, and community partners. The mission statement is an opportunity to articulate the core values of the organization and the vision that it has for the world and its work in the world.

Mission statements must be reviewed periodically to ensure that they are still relevant and an accurate reflection of the organization and its work. When reviewing it, make sure that it reflects the organization's current vision and language. It should never be viewed as a "historical" document. The question to ask is: "Does our organization's mission statement still address issues that are of concern in today's world?"

Often the mission is identical to the original impulse that inspired the creation of the organization and reflects the community needs identified years earlier. Sometimes the same problems haunt generation after generation, and the organization's purpose does not change—although how it does business very likely has evolved. Sometimes the purpose of the organization has changed as times have changed. Even 5 or 10 years can change the social landscape so dramatically that the original mission must be updated, altered modestly, or changed dramatically to address new realities. For example, the March of Dimes was originally created to stamp out polio. Now it fights against a broader array of debilitating illnesses affecting children. See Exhibit 3.1 to understand how the March of Dimes has changed its name and mission over time.

Task One: Review the Organization's Mission Statement

Before beginning the strategic communications planning process, an organization should confirm that the mission statement is current and an accurate reflection of what it stands for and what it is trying to achieve. This is also an appropriate time to evaluate whether the mission statement expresses the organization's purpose clearly and concisely. A good mission

Exhibit 3.1 March of Dimes: Evolution of a Name and Mission

Date	Action	Mission
1938	Franklin D. Roosevelt establishes the National Foundation for Infantile Paralysis	The National Foundation for Infantile Paralysis is a national, public nonprofit that raises funds for polio research and to care for those suffering from the disease.
1952	Jonas Salk tests a vaccine on 1.8 million Polio Pioneers, the largest public health inoculation program in history; polio abates dramatically	
1958		Our mission is to improve the health of babies by preventing birth defects, premature birth and infant mortality.
1962	Albert Sabin tests the oral polio vaccine, further reducing incidences of polio in the United States	
1979	The Foundation changes its name to the March of Dimes, highlighting the name associated with its major annual fundraising drive	Slogan ``Saving Babies Together''

statement should explain why the organization exists and what it hopes to achieve in the future. A vital mission statement also articulates the essential nature of an organization, its values, and its work and defines the environment in which the organization exists.

At the very least, the organization's mission statement should answer three fundamental questions:

1. What are the opportunities or needs that we exist to address? (the *purpose* of the organization)
2. What are we doing to address them? (the *business* of the organization)
3. What ability and experience do we have to meet these needs? (the *values* of the organization)

Here are three mission statements that answer these questions.

Caring Connections

Caring Connections provides information to help people talk with loved ones, ask questions of their doctors, and understand the range of issues involved in care at the end of life.

- The *purpose* is to help people make informed decisions about end-of-life care.
- The *business* is providing information to inform those decisions.
- The *values* support informed decision making so people can have the treatments they desire and the comfort of knowing they are in command of their care at the end of life.

The National Conference

The National Conference, founded in 1927 as the National Conference of Christians and Jews, is a human relations organization dedicated to fighting bias, bigotry, and racism in America. The National Conference promotes understanding and respect among all races, religions, and cultures through advocacy, conflict resolution, and education.

- The *purpose* is to fight bias, bigotry, and racism in America.
- The *business* is to advocate, resolve conflicts, and provide education.
- The *values* are a commitment to understanding and respect among all races, religions, and cultures.

Planet 3000

Planet 3000 is committed to healing the earth. Using research into natural ecosystems, Planet 3000 develops policy recommendations and pilot projects that apply these principles to human ecosystems such as cultural habits, social structures, commercial ventures, and other projects. It advocates for the establishment of human ecosystems that are in harmony with other life on the planet. By bringing the human social order into balance with ecological principles, diversity of all living things can be sustained and the evolutionary process that has guided and nurtured life on this planet for millions of years can continue unabated.

- The *purpose* is to heal the planet.
- The *business* is to advocate, support research, and foster demonstration projects.
- The *values* are based in ecological principles: balance, diversity, recognition of the evolutionary process, and advancing harmony with life on the planet.

Recently, organizations have begun to move toward shorter mission statements, 20 to 25 words in length, which could more accurately be described as organization descriptions. This change is in recognition of the need to have concise spoken language that can be used across the organization by all those who are associated with it. The organization description fits well in conversations and Web communications. If the organization has not replaced its mission statement with this shorter format, it should consider crafting an organization statement to supplement its mission statement. Tips for creating an organization description can be found in Chapter 7.

In either case, the organization needs to ensure that the mission statement and the organization description are free of jargon and easily understood by those outside the organization's normal field. The organization's mission statement must rally the troops. To do this, it must resonate with the people who work in and for the organization as well as with each of the different constituencies the organization hopes to reach. It must express the organization's purpose in a way that inspires commitment, passion, innovation, and courage. The mission statement is the foundation of the entire message platform for nonprofit organizations.

Worksheet 5, found at the end of this chapter, can be used to state or recreate the mission statement and to restate the goals as a quick reference and reminder for the CAT.

Task Two: Review the Organization's Program Goals, Objectives, and Financial Priorities

A strategic plan addresses the key program areas, development efforts, and major accomplishments the organization hopes to achieve in order to realize its vision and fulfill its mission. In addition to the communications plan, key components of an organization's strategic plan that provide important information to shape the strategic communications plan include:

- Financial plan, including strategies for sustaining the organization 10 years into the future
- Program and operations plan
- Technology plan for supporting business priorities
- Development plans, covering both donated funds and earned income
- Organizational development and human resources plan
- Board development and leadership succession plans

The strategic planning process focuses on the critical issues facing the nonprofit organization and the core strategies for addressing those issues. Defining operational goals and objectives and monitoring organizational progress toward meeting those goals and objectives is central to strategic planning.

A program goal should answer these questions:

- What impact or change does the organization want to happen?
- What will it take to make that happen?
- Who will the organization serve or influence by doing this?

In addition to external program goals, organizations also can have internal management or functional goals. Although these may not seem directly related to the organization's mission, they often play a critical role in its ultimate success and may affect the allocation of the organization's resources. For example, an organization might have the goal of maintaining accurate and current financial information in a way that is easily accessible to key staff and board members in order to maximize the use of financial resources. Or internal management or functional goals could include a commitment to develop and nurture an enthusiastic, committed, and well-informed staff able to function well in interdisciplinary teams.

Rules of the Road: Tips for Preparing to Plan

1. **The CAT leader should compile all appropriate documents** to support the strategic communications planning process:
   - Previous communications plans, if any.
   - Strategic plan.
   - Financial plan.
   - Program and operational plan.
   - Technology plan.
   - Fundraising plan.
   - Organizational development plan (including human resources).
   - Board development and leadership succession plans.
2. **The CAT reviews the mission statement.** Remember that a mission statement should:
   - Serve to define who you are, making clear what is unique about what you do.
   - Contain inspiring language to elicit passionate support and on-going commitment.

- Be grounded in the past and project that history into the future, articulated in a way that is easy to understand.
- Be free of jargon or philosophical statements and use clear, simple, straightforward language.
- Be concise, so that all who read your mission statement can easily recall the essence of what your organization does.

3. **The CAT reviews the strategic planning goals and the findings of the communications audit.** Remember that the project goals should:
   - Grow out of the organization's mission.
   - Reflect priority initiatives.
   - Specify the desired outcomes for the organization, consider the strategies to be pursued, and identify those who will be affected.
   - Be strategic in their focus with the goal of having long-term impact.
   - Collectively, comprise the organization's realistic priorities.

4. **The CAT identifies the communications challenges** inherent in the project goals:
   - Be specific about what is to be accomplished and the desired outcomes.
   - Identify the stakeholders and target audiences to be addressed.
   - Set specific targets, measured either quantitatively or qualitatively, that can be used to assess progress along the way.
   - Always set target dates for accomplishing your communications objectives.

Communications Audit

When the communications function seems out of step with the rest of the organization's work, it is not always easy to pinpoint where the problem lies. Questions arise when the board and/or staff feel that the organization's communications are not as effective as they could be, or when a communication fails to generate the desired response or results, or when the organization receives complaints from key stakeholders about its communications efforts: Why did the material fail to resonate with the target audience? Is the problem with the message? Is the problem with the means of communication? Does the fault lie with the messenger? Was too much time spent on the production and not enough on the actual content of the piece?

In examining its communications work, an organization may find that it makes use of too many vehicles to communicate with its varied customer bases, partners, members, and other key constituencies. Too much time and effort may be required to maintain and update these vehicles on a routine basis. Sometimes it is not clear which vehicles are most effective in conveying needed information to solicit the desired response. Web sites and portals, listservs, e-mail discussion groups, e-newsletters, bulletin boards, blogs, vlogs (video blogs), and instant messaging require technical expertise and regular, almost daily, staff attention. And new communications vehicles and tools are being developed every day. Connecting with key audiences requires familiarity and expertise in using each of these tools and techniques, individually and in concert with each other. But more important, communications activities must add up to more than the sum of their parts or they become a series of isolated events. Being strategic requires that an organization is deliberate, savvy, and innovative in a manner that maximizes all of its communications work.

Nonprofit organizations are becoming much more strategic in their appreciation of the value of effective communications, but many questions remain about their actual capacity to implement these strategies in the face of their many priorities and limited resources. To ensure that they are putting their resources into the areas that most need attention, organizations should conduct a communications audit prior to launching the strategic communications planning process. Communications audits are also necessary during times of crisis or transition, when external circumstances affecting the organization have changed, or when an organization goes through a merger. *A communications audit is a comprehensive analysis of an organization's communications—internal and/or external—to review communications needs, policies, practices, and capacity in order to improve organization efficiency and effectiveness.*

A communications audit should be conducted routinely every five to seven years, simply to ensure that the organization is staying current with trends, changing language, new communications vehicles and techniques and to update design elements. In the interim, the organization can rely on information gathered via the monitoring and evaluation mechanisms instituted as part of the strategic communications plan. Staff assessments, readership surveys, focus groups, and board reviews can also provide helpful information for midcourse corrections.

Worksheet 6, found at the end of this chapter, can be used to help summarize the findings of the communications audit to guide the work of the CAT.

Purpose of the Communications Audit

A communications audit typically serves four purposes:

1. It serves as a review of the organization's communications to determine utility, cost effectiveness, and success in reaching current and prospective constituencies. It provides valuable data to help the nonprofit develop or restructure its communications functions, guidelines, and budgets.

2. It assesses current and potential vehicles to ensure that the organization's needs are being met through a review of content, vehicles, frequency, media utilization, and communications delivery mechanisms. It assesses the existing communications programs, communications vehicles, and outreach techniques used to reach key constituencies, including relevance, appropriateness, and timeliness of communications. Content analysis determines the organization's effectiveness in communicating about the organization in general, promoting program and services, and/or related to the handling of a specific issue or circumstance.

3. It addresses how the organization approaches its communications work. It evaluates the organization's communications philosophy, any formal policies, the structure and relationship between communications staff and management, and the relationship between communications to other staff functions and to the organization's operations, in general. The audit reviews organizational staffing and compensation, including contracts with outside vendors and consultants, the roles and responsibilities of each, and the process for edit and review functions during production.

4. It informs the strategic communications plan, especially those components that have to do with internal communications and plan implementation. It assesses the communications relationships within the organization and between the organization and its constituencies. It evaluates the operational framework for communications within the organization. It determines what is working well, what is not, and what might work better if adjustments are made.

Finally, the communications audit must be placed in the context of the needs and expectations of the board and leadership. What concerns are prompting a review of the communications function? What are the prevailing attitudes toward the organization's existing communications activities? What needs to be addressed to improve the quantity, quality and reliability of the information supporting the mission of the organization?

Components of a Communications Audit

An audit generally consists of:

- Personal interviews with constituents/members, donors/funders, policy makers/partners, and other key stakeholders to determine if the nonprofit's communications are successfully informing and engaging them
- A review of existing communications for content, messaging and design effectiveness
- A review of existing communications vehicles to understand how they meet the needs of the audience
- A review of existing communications management to ascertain cost effectiveness in the areas of content, editorial review, design, and production

The final product is a report that identifies and addresses gaps, including recommendations and strategies for improving performance and strengthening the communications between the organization and its constituencies. This report ensures that the organization is providing the right information, to the right people, in the right format, at the right time, with the right result.

Conducting the Communications Audit: Methodology

Task One: Plan the Audit

The communications action team (CAT) must determine the objectives for the communications audit, identify key question areas, gather essential information, plan an approach, and develop a schedule. The same roles and responsibilities that guide the strategic communications planning process will be applied to the audit. If a separate communications audit team will be assuming responsibility for the communication audit, roles and responsibilities must be clearly identified and an action plan, timeline, and regular reporting mechanisms must be developed.

The communications audit team should determine how it intends to gather information about the current performance and capacity of the organization. Traditionally, this step includes interviews with senior management, board members, and targeted key stakeholders outside of the organization. The team should determine how many interviews it intends to conduct, develop the list of interviewees, and design a standard survey instrument. Questions introduced in Chapter 1 may prove helpful in developing the survey.

Task Two: Conduct Interviews

The CAT or audit team conducts interviews with top management and key internal stakeholders to determine management's attitudes and beliefs about communication as well as to pinpoint communications problems. These interviews help identify organizational and management issues, as well as flaws in the actual communications vehicles. It also suggests areas for additional research and can help narrow the focus of the communications audit.

Audit questions should be tailored for each audience and will be different for the board, senior management, and key stakeholders. Typical questions might be:

- What do you think is most unique about the organization?
- What does the organization do especially well in its communications with you? With others who are active and support the organization?
- What could the organization do better in its communications?
- What is the most compelling reason to support the organization?
- Do the organization's advertising and communications stand out from its peers?
- What is the organization's current membership/marketing campaign? What do you think of it?
- Are the organization's products and services clearly promoted?
- Are there other issues regarding the organization that you would like to raise?

Task Three: Inventory and Analysis

The audit team collects, inventories, and analyzes the communications products developed by the organization, including all existing communications materials, communications vehicles and programs, media kits, letterhead, fact sheets, brochures, publications, audiovisuals, Web material, and any other collateral materials used by the organization. Through this process, the true strengths and weaknesses of the organization's current communications become apparent.

Communications Materials.   The inventory and analysis of current communications vehicles is an opportunity for involving staff in the strategic communications planning process. The CAT or audit team gathers all of the print material that the organization currently uses and places it face-up on the largest table available. The materials should include everything from business cards and letterhead to brochures, annual reports, fact sheets, membership applications, magazines and other publications, print versions of key pages from the Web sites, videos, and other vehicles. The CAT then determines the answers to the following questions:

Do the pieces look similar?

Do they look like they came from the same organization?

Do they use the same basic design elements: type fonts, type size, colors, layout, use of pictures, graphics, and illustrations?

What pieces are most dramatic? What pieces seem lackluster or dull? Why?

Do the pieces carry the same basic information about the organization: mission statement, vision, 25-word organization description, and descriptions of programs and services?

Are there pictures, graphics, and illustrations? Are these used in a consistent manner? What is missing, if anything? What could be better?

Does the organization have a style manual for its publications? Is it routinely followed in the communications practices of the organization? (See Appendix 3 for a discussion of Style Manuals.)

Web Site Usability Testing.   Online communication is proactive, interactive, and ongoing. The first test of an effective Web site is whether the information is light, layered, and linked. It provides information in a well-written and well maintained presence (light), involves finding, cross referencing, and posting relevant information (layered), and identifies and connects with other relevant sites (linked).

From a content perspective,

- Does it present all of the organization's essential information in a manner that quickly meets needs of the user, and, at the same time, invites users to browse and learn more about the nonprofit organization and its work?

Second, to be effective, a Web site must meet the communications and strategic needs of the nonprofit organization and be easy to navigate for the staff and the user. The site must be both user and usage centered. User-centered design ensures that the Web site meets the information needs of the constituents it serves. Usage-centered design ensures that the organization is structuring the information available on the site so that it supports the nonprofit's needs: processing requests for information, automating conference and workshop registration, online advocacy, and donations and/or membership registration.

From an operational standpoint:

- Is the Web site easy to maintain and update?
- Does the Web site permit visitors to do what they want with little or no assistance?
- Does the Web site accommodate additional content areas and allow new functionalities to be added without major restructuring?
- Is it a good platform that integrates several communications functions (i.e., e-newsletters, videos, chat rooms, etc.)?
- Is it interactive and able to promote automated services, such as online registration for workshops?
- Does it encourage users to share and exchange experiences, ideas, and knowledge?

A quick review of the Web site will help the team evaluate whether it meets the standards of user-centered and usage-centered design.

Task Four: Present Findings

As the key issues around the organization's communications efforts begin to surface, the audit team should meet with the CAT to present findings to date, to consider the implications for the strategic communications plan, and to discuss areas that require additional research. The communications audit should result in more than just lists of things that work, things that do not work, and things that should be improved. To ensure that the recommendations and audit findings will be used and that actual practice will be improved, the audit should:

- Demonstrate through data how communications problems are causing problems *in the present* (as opposed to speculating about their future impact). At the same time, the audit should reinforce practices that are current organizational strengths.
- Generate specific recommendations for *how* actual communication practice can be enhanced. Data need to be linked to concrete actions.
- Make transparent the organizational benefits of adopting those actions in addition to the weaknesses they are designed to address.
- Prioritize recommendations so organizations are not immobilized by the prospect of implementing them.[1]

[1]O. Hargie and D. Tourish, *Handbook of Communication Audits for Organizations* (London: Routledge, 2000).

For ease of implementation, it might be handy to identify those recommendations that can be implemented immediately with little investment of time or resources; those that may require some planning and testing but could be implemented in the near term; and those that (either due to requirements of significant effort or additional resources) will become longer-term initiatives to be included in the strategic communications plan.

Task Five: Conduct Additional Research (Optional)

If the audit team and the CAT decide that additional research is necessary, focus groups or surveys of key constituents may be needed. The input of members, clients, coalition or partnering organizations, community leaders, and others can be extremely valuable to help define new directions, new messages, new vehicles, and new methods of communication. The audit team develops a research strategy that includes targeting the audience, developing the survey instrument, administering the research, tabulating and summarizing the results, and presenting the key findings to the board and staff.

Rules of the Road: Conduct a Communications Audit

1. The CAT should determine if a communications audit is necessary. It can conduct the audit itself or form a separate communications audit team. Remember that the communications audit:
   - Reviews the current communications work (production).
   - Assesses current and potential vehicles for content and effectiveness (product design).
   - Evaluates the policies and organizational structure supporting all communications activity (management).
   - Informs the strategic communications plan.
2. The Audit Team or the CAT should refer issues regarding organizational structure, the need for better interdepartmental coordination, staffing needs, and other management issues to the senior management team.

Worksheet 5   Mission Statement and Goals

Name of Organization: _____

Mission Statement

Goals
1.
2.
3.

Worksheet 6   Communications Audit Summary

Step 1. Decide whether the organization has been effective or not effective in performing this function.

Step 2. Rank the five most critical steps for the success of this strategic communications planning process for your organization at this time. Check the appropriate boxes.

Category	Not Effective	Effective	Rank the Top 5
Communications Policy			
a. Clear mission, goals, and strategic plan	1 2 3	4 5	
b. Strong brand and design identity	1 2 3	4 5	
c. Clear messages and language platform	1 2 3	4 5	
c. Clear, consistent logo, images, and visuals	1 2 3	4 5	
d. Effective media relations plan	1 2 3	4 5	
e. Strong Web site	1 2 3	4 5	
f. Effective membership/ outreach strategy	1 2 3	4 5	
g. Clearly identified audiences including their information needs	1 2 3	4 5	
Communications Practices			
a. Board support for communications	1 2 3	4 5	
b. Senior management support for communications	1 2 3	4 5	

c. Cost effective; sufficient financial resources	1 2 3	4 5	
d. Communications fully integrated into every program, project, and strategy	1 2 3	4 5	
e. Most staff members have some knowledge and participate in the communications efforts	1 2 3	4 5	
f. Clear editorial policy including roles and responsibilities for who writes, who edits, and who has final approval of content	1 2 3	4 5	
Communications Capacity/Production			
a. Experienced and reliable staff	1 2 3	4 5	
b. Competent vendors and consultants	1 2 3	4 5	
c. Strong production team	1 2 3	4 5	
d. Clear production guidelines	1 2 3	4 5	
e. Style guide consistently implemented	1 2 3	4 5	
f. Web site has user-centered design	1 2 3	4 5	
g. Web site has usage-centered design	1 2 3	4 5	

4

Step Two: Foundation of the Plan
The Situation Analysis

Effective communication starts with a clear understanding of the environment in which the organization functions. Every organization should conduct periodically an *environmental scan* or *analysis*, sometimes known as a *situation analysis*. The purpose of an environmental analysis is to help key players within your organization define the playing field and gain information about the forces that will influence the communications plan.

A comprehensive environmental analysis looks at areas both inside and outside the organization. The internal analysis examines the organization's operations and identifies strengths and weaknesses (SW). The external analysis examines forces that influence every organization, looking for opportunities and threats (OT). This SWOT analysis provides critical information for the successful implementation of the strategic communications plan.

The challenges for the communications action team (CAT) are to:

- Accumulate information that will allow members to understand the current and previous strategies of the organization
- Assess the organization's programs, their effectiveness and competitive position
- Determine the opportunities and challenges relative to the needs of key stakeholders and those they serve
- Identify any additional strategic issues or challenges that may exist[1]

---

[1]Michael Allison and Jude Kaye, *Strategic Planning for Nonprofit Organizations: A Practical Guide and Workbook* (Hoboken, NJ: John Wiley & Sons, 2005), p. 75.

Internal Analysis

The internal analysis focuses on the operations inside the organization to better understand what is desired of it and what is possible, given available resources and tools. This analysis looks at the organization's culture and structure, program and management objectives, human and financial resources, and physical and technological infrastructure. A basic tenet of the strategic communications planning model is that all senior managers need to understand the importance of internal and external communications. By examining these pieces of the puzzle, the staff and board should be able to understand not only what is possible but also what is permissible given this set of facts.

An organization's administrative structure may have served it well for the last 25 years, but, over time, management responsibilities or program changes may indicate a need to restructure communication responsibilities. For example, the current structure may not permit the easy flow of information and work among team members from various departments with different supervisors and competing departmental priorities. Furthermore, an appreciation of the organization's culture will also influence how bold or how cautious it will be when planning its strategies and tactics for advancing the mission. Staff morale will have an effect on team members' commitment to innovation, restructuring, and the potential need to expand or downsize. When an organization's management objectives conflict with its program objectives, the reconciliation of these two factors has an impact on staff. If the organization is financially sound, it can expand programming. But if the financial situation is tight, cuts will have to be made and personnel will be affected. Similarly, if the organization understands how to maximize its human and technological resources, it may be able to work in a more cost-effective manner.

Organizational Culture

An effective strategic communications plan must be an accurate reflection of the organization's culture. It must reflect the current working relationships, partnerships, performance expectations, and organizational framework. If the plan addresses the current infrastructure, it must also include communications strategies to help board, staff, and other key constituencies understand and support the desired change of direction.

Among the questions to consider:

- How much autonomy do staff members have in their work?
- Is there a relatively free flow of information within the organization, or do people tend not to share?

- What is the attitude at the organization—is it open and friendly, scared and paranoid, cynical?
- Do staff members feel that they are treated fairly?
- Are there clear reporting relationships and a common understanding of how departments work with each other?
- Are there interdepartmental teams that meet on a regular basis?
- Are there any areas where responsibilities overlap?

Once the CAT has a clear understanding of these core organizational values, it can determine whether it will work within these parameters or try to institute change. The use of the strategic communications planning model, which assumes the use of a short-term interdepartmental working group, can be a catalyst for new working relationships for the nonprofit organization.

In addition to understanding the organization's culture, a common strategic planning approach to the internal analysis of an organization is to examine the organization's strengths and weaknesses in five areas:

1. Administration
2. Programs
3. Human resources
4. Infrastructure
5. Development

Working with the board and staff, the CAT should identify the organization's strengths and weaknesses in each of these five areas. If the CAT conducts this exercise independently, it should share the findings with the senior management team to ensure that they understand and agree with the interpretation and assumptions reached by the CAT. The senior management team may decide to address some of the issues separately to ensure that the CAT can plan strategies to address the organization's weaknesses and make the best use of its strengths within the communications context (see Exhibit 4.1).

Administration

The active support of the senior management team, including its commitment to the overall strategic plan, its promotion of the mission and purpose, and its recognition that communications is essential to all aspects of the nonprofit's work, helps create an environment of success for the strategic communications plan. Senior managers need to embrace the plan and encourage their departments to act on the findings and recommendations in the plan. Many a plan has died on the shelf because those with the power to make sure it happened were not brought into the process soon enough, failed to make an active commitment to the plan, or quietly sabotaged the plan.

Often the administrative structure of an organization has not kept pace with evolving priorities. Evaluating administrative processes and departmental or committee structures, and reshaping them when necessary, can help the nonprofit organization to operate more efficiently to meet its goals. Uniting around the strategic communications planning and implementation processes can help model new approaches to the work of the organization. In this way, they help the organization to understand that the plan will influence what work gets done and how it gets done in the future.

Programs

Effective communications strategies can ensure that key constituencies are being connected with the programs and services that they need. A close look at your programs will reveal which ones are thriving (highest donor support, most clients, greatest activist response) and which seem to be faltering. Program staff members should be actively solicited to participate in the strategic communications planning process and to help the CAT understand what works well and what could work better. Determining the root causes of these strengths and weaknesses can help you tailor new communications objectives to improve the overall success of program promotion and outreach.

Human Resources

Organizations are all about the people involved and the kinds of skills and resources they bring to the table. In the broadest sense, the organization's human resources include not just staff but also board members, volunteers, donors, and advocates. What types of human resources does the organization need, and how can it make the best use of what is available to it? The strategic communications process provides an opportunity to engage all of the organization's human resources in a way that can revitalize the nonprofit and its commitment to its mission. Perhaps the current suite of skills (and attitudes!) could be improved through training or recruitment. Helping staff, volunteers, and the board support the implementation of the strategic communications plan could be an important planning component of CAT's work.

Infrastructure

To some extent, the nonprofit's infrastructure determines how well positioned it is to meet program goals and implement communications objectives. Is the physical environment (e.g., availability of parking, security, signage, space for confidential discussions) adequate to meet the needs of staff members and clients? Does the organization have the equipment (e.g., enough phone lines and computer workstations, up-to-date software and databases) to get the job done? Are there common working spaces, meeting rooms, and other centers to allow for all staff members to be engaged and involved in the critical work being done?

Development

The term *development* is more than a euphemism for bringing in the money to fund operations. *Development* refers to the need to reach out and cultivate, or *develop*, relationships that will help the nonprofit organization build a solid financial foundation.

A new nonprofit organization may start by relying on a small pool of funders that provide hefty start-up grants. As these grants run their course or the organization begins to thrive, the organization will be best served by developing a diversified base of financial support that includes private individuals, private foundations, and corporations along with income streams generated by the organization.

Large nonprofit organizations with diversified funding sources face different communications challenges as they try to ensure that donors continue to provide support. Donors must get enough of the right information at the right intervals to keep them informed and involved with the organization. The information needs of foundations and granting organizations are not the same as those of corporations and individual donors.

The CAT must work with development staff to understand their communications priorities and to consider how the strategic communications plan can support relationships with key financial stakeholders.

Rules of the Road: Internal Analysis

1. The CAT should conduct a review of the organization culture and the five key areas of the internal analysis. For best results, the CAT should meet with high-level staff and at least one influential board member.
2. The CAT should examine the information and data already on hand (e.g., from ongoing measurement efforts) and identify areas that require further research.
3. The CAT should consider organizing a town meeting or focus group with staff or other key constituents (e.g., clients, donors, representatives of partner organizations) to solicit their views of the organization's strengths and weaknesses.
4. The CAT should identify key challenges that must be incorporated into the strategic communications plan to build on the internal strengths and to address weaknesses.

External Analysis

The external analysis examines the macro-environment—the world in which the nonprofit organization functions every day. Just as it is important for the CAT to understand the internal forces that will influence the strategic communications plan, it must consider the external environment. The more an organization knows and understands about the environment in which it is working, the better it can craft strategies, target audiences, and develop messages that will bring success.

As part of this process, looking at the *competition*—that is, other organizations with missions similar to the organization's—can be instructive. A simple exercise is to identify the groups and individuals that actively compete for the same audiences and support that the nonprofit seeks to influence. These competitor organizations may provide similar programs and services, or they may be perceived as doing the same things—whether that is true or not. Understanding where the nonprofit sits in comparison to other similar organizations is an important part of the branding and positioning work.

Worksheet 7, found at the end of this chapter, can be used to conduct the situation analysis of internal and external forces.

The external analysis typically addresses the macro-environment. New opportunities or problems will develop as these forces change over time. The challenge for the organization is to be prepared to take advantage of emerging possibilities and to meet or avoid threats with carefully prepared contingency plans. By examining these outside forces, the organization will have a clear picture of where it stands and can be prepared to take advantage of new opportunities. Five outside forces pose opportunities and threats (OT) to the nonprofit organization:

1. Demographic forces
2. Economic forces
3. Political forces
4. Technological forces
5. Social forces

Demographic Forces

Changes in the population that the organization serves (e.g., aging residents, a baby boom, influxes of new immigrants) may place new demands on organizational resources, services, and staff or require a refocusing of the organization's mission or service delivery. An influx of new residents may create new target groups for programs and services or tax existing programs by pulling resources away from other important work of the organization. Anticipating where these changes may occur will make the organization more effective in serving those in need.

Economic Forces

Changing economic indicators (e.g., rising or shrinking unemployment rates) may increase demand for existing services or suggest new service opportunities. A healthy economy may increase donor support or present an opportunity to diversify the funding base; a decline in the economy may signal a need to slow down program expansion and possibly redeploy some resources.

Political Forces

The traditional "business" of nonprofits is increasingly tied to policy making at all levels. Consider the effect of healthcare or welfare reform, communications deregulation, environmental policy, or foreign aid, and it is easy to see how connected the fates of nonprofits and foundations are to the political environment. On particular issues, the leadership may change from the federal government to state or local government, or vice versa. Being politically aware can help the nonprofit take advantage of effective partnering with local political leaders to advance its social agenda.

Technological Forces

Advances in technology can create new, cost-effective ways to relate to different audiences, do research, track grants, and compile and analyze information. Technology is making it possible for constituents to access programs and services electronically, increasing the organization's service base with minimal effort.

Social Forces

Nonprofits focus on the human condition—what the public perceives as the critical aspects of human behavior that affect the quality of life. Changes in the social agenda can present both opportunities and challenges for nonprofits. Over the last 20 years, for example, increased demands on our time, the increase in professionals who are retiring early and want to give back, and disasters and other events have changed the face of volunteering in the United States.

Although the organization cannot control these environmental forces, it *can* stay abreast of trends, crises, and new developments. The organization can work to influence developments in the external environment in ways that will advance its mission, not hinder it. The key is to identify and understand these external forces and to develop appropriate responses to them.

Rules of the Road: Tips for Connecting with the External Environment

1. Encourage the CAT to stay informed about current affairs through newspapers, specialized publications, government reports, and news services.
2. Senior management should conduct informal discussion groups once or twice a year with people who represent various constituencies or organizational stakeholders: board members, clients, activists, community leaders, pollsters, academics, and the like. These discussion groups can help confirm or challenge the CAT's estimate of where outside forces are heading and their anticipated effects on the organization.
3. Senior management can use written or telephone surveys to gain insights into public opinion or targeted population attitudes. The surveys can be conducted by a professional firm or by volunteers and staff members. The quality of the questions is the key to a useful survey. Be sure that the questions are clear, specific, and thorough.
4. Senior management can conduct in-depth interviews with a small number of individuals who are representative of the targeted audiences to identify critical needs and/or explore specific responses to different strategies or solutions.

SWOT Analysis

Once the situation analysis has been completed, the CAT should meet to review the results and consider the strategic implications within it. The external analysis should reveal where the organization is meeting the needs of key stakeholders and where it may have been out of touch or need to revise and improve its outreach and communications efforts. It may also reveal significant new opportunities for expansion or a change in focus for the nonprofit. It may suggest that there is significant competition for some major clients and constituencies or suggest that there are new constituencies in great need of the services provided by the organization.

The planning tool used to evaluate the findings in the situation analysis is called a SWOT analysis, where SWOT refers to the Strengths, Weaknesses,

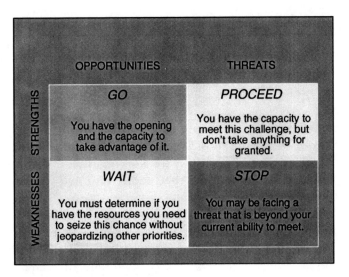

Exhibit 4.1 SWOT Analysis

Opportunities, and Threats that confront an organization. Within the internal audit, the analysis looked at the organization's culture and structure, program and management objectives, human and financial resources, and physical and technological infrastructure. By examining these pieces of the puzzle, the staff and board should be able to understand not only what is possible but also what is permissible. The internal audit reveals the organization's strengths and weaknesses. Examination of the external environment will enable the organization to identify opportunities and to develop contingency plans to avoid or lessen the impact of any threat or disadvantageous situations on the horizon.

As a team, the CAT members should review the findings in the situation analysis and discuss the internal audit to determine the organization's strengths and weaknesses. The CAT should then review the external audit and determine the areas of opportunity and the potential threats on the horizon. Because of the strategic implications of this step in the process, the senior management team and the board leaders must participate in this process or, at a minimum, carefully review the findings and recommendations of the CAT.

Once the four components have been identified and consensus has been reached about the most significant factors, the CAT should develop a grid to help the organization determine where its greatest opportunities for achieving its mission, advancing its programs and positions, and/or serving the greatest number of constituents are. Worksheet 8 is designed to help an organization determine where it should focus its energies.

Worksheet 8, found at the end of this chapter, can be used to help conduct the SWOT analysis.

Consider, for example, an organization with a strong structure that has kept its employees working in silos. Every team works in a vacuum, and there is duplication of effort. The opportunity for working in interdisciplinary teams has been identified as something that could improve the organization's communications across the programs, services, membership, and donor relations. To achieve the desired results, the administrative structure of the organization may have to change—for example, a new structure may be required to organize the flow of information and the setting of work priorities among interdisciplinary teams, members of which come from several different departments with different supervisors with different priorities. The success of this new structure will require strong leadership at the top, consensus among senior managers that this is the right path to follow, team-building exercises, and other work and planning sessions.

Similarly, say an organization discovers that a key demographic group in its community could benefit from its programs and services. The organization must carefully review existing programs and services and must develop and implement a marketing and outreach plan. Decisions will need to be made about the redeployment of existing resources, and some programs and services may need to be cut or reduced to free up personnel and resources to move in the new direction. The human and other resource issues that emerge from such restructuring must be handled to achieve success.

Some changes may be too drastic for the organization to address, especially in the near term. Using the graph in Exhibit 4.1, the CAT can determine whether to redeploy resources or whether the challenges are too great and may threaten the survival of the organization. Opportunities that draw on an organization's strengths might be pursued. Opportunities that draw on an organization's weaknesses may require too much resource redeployment. Similarly, if a threat in the community draws on the organization's strengths, the nonprofit may be able to redeploy resources and emerge from the challenge stronger and better positioned within the community. However, if a threat in the community seems insurmountable, given the nonprofit's weaknesses, the smarter strategy may be to ignore the threat and to focus all of the organization's efforts on an area in which it is strong and where opportunity exists. Worksheet 9 can help you to see how each of these factors is intertwined and what is actually possible and what contributes to the organization's long-term sustainability.

Worksheet 9, found at the end of this chapter, can be used to evaluate the SWOT and set strategic direction for the communications plan.

Critical Community Partners and Stakeholders

Once the CAT has clearly reviewed all the strategic priorities for the organization and identified the environment surrounding the development of the plan, it should invite the board, senior staff, or others involved in the plan to participate in an exercise to define the broad network of community partners and stakeholders that the organization touches. Although every member or category within this network will not be tapped to support the strategic objectives, this exercise will ensure that no individual or party is inadvertently overlooked. The other major benefit of this exercise is that it helps the CAT recognize the full range of resources that can potentially be tapped to help achieve the plan's objectives.

Once the CAT has completed its analysis of the SWOT findings, it will have identified the strategic initiatives that will become the foundation for the strategic communications plan. It can then tackle its work to define the audiences, develop the messages and communications strategies, and consider how to measure impact.

Worksheet 10, found at the end of this chapter, can be used to identify the community partners and stakeholders that should be considered when building the communications plan.

Rules of the Road: Creating the Strategic Framework

1. The CAT should review the internal and external analysis, the organizational culture, and the SWOT analysis in the context of the strategic planning goals and the communications challenges that were identified in Chapter 3.
2. The CAT must reach consensus on the priorities for the next five years. This is a strategic moment to share the work of the CAT with senior management and, possibly, the board. It is the nonprofit that must commit to these priorities before the CAT can decide who needs to be reached, what needs to be done, and how best to persuade these target audiences to take the desired actions.

Worksheet 7   Situation Analysis

Examining the External Environment

Demographic Forces: Who are the primary groups that benefit from the organization? Has there been a shift or change in the populations or the makeup of the communities that it serves? If yes, what does that mean? If no, is that cause for alarm?

Economic Forces: What are the sources of revenue for the organization? Is it sufficiently diversified? How do donors perceive the organization, and what does that mean for its financial future (consider government funding, foundations and corporate contributors)? Is the economy shifting in ways that will cause growth or decline in demand for services from the populations that the organization serves?

Technological Forces: What are the latest trends in business technology that might allow the organization to be more effective? What are the latest products or trends in online technology that could impact the work: program development, technical assistance, volunteer recruitment, training, education, etc.? How will recent trends in communications technology affect the organization? Does the organization need to improve its technology to create a better product, improve services, conduct more cost-effective advocacy efforts?

Political Forces: How do current political priorities influence the organization and its work? What will be on the national, local, and state political agenda this year? Could it affect the organization or the populations that it serves? If the winds blow our way, what can we expect? If they go against us, what is the worst that can happen? Is there something we are not seeing?

Social Forces: What social or cultural trends are occurring in the community, state, and nation? What does this mean for the organization and its work? What social or cultural values are embraced by the constituents we serve? Have these values changed recently? If so, why? Does that impact the organization's relationship to its constituents? What is the mood of the nation? Of the community? What is the latest fear in society? What is the latest demand? What is the latest "hope" or "solution" being talked about? How could these fears, demands, and hopes impact the organization?

Examining the Internal Environment

Management Objectives: Is there a strategic plan that guides the work of the organization? Are there clear management objectives? Is staff aware of the management objectives of the organization and what that means for their job performance? How do they relate to program objectives? Has the organization defined what each management objective means and why it is important for the organization's success? Are there mechanisms for staff input or feedback?

Human Resources: What expertise does the staff have? What knowledge base resides in the staff? Do we provide training for staff? Do we have staff expertise in all the areas on which the organization is focused? Do we have too many or not enough volunteers for the programs that require volunteer involvement? What additional staffing do we require?

Financial Resources: Is the organization on sound financial footing? Does its financial resources cover existing activities? Does the organization pay its expenses in a timely manner? Does the organization have a reserve fund? Does it have a core group of supporters and donors? Does this base need to be expanded? diversified?

Physical Infrastructure: Does the organization have enough workspace for staff, consultants, and temporary workers? Is the space conducive to teamwork? Is there adequate light, air, heat? Can people have a private conversation if they need to? Is the neighborhood safe for staff working odd hours? Is there room to expand if the organization takes on new programs?

Technology Infrastructure: Do people have adequate computers and software to perform their jobs? Does the phone system meet the needs of the organization? Are there other special equipment needs that should be addressed?

Worksheet 8   Strengths, Weaknesses, Opportunities, Threats

What are the strengths of the organization?

What are the weaknesses of the organization?

What opportunities exist in the next 18 months?

What threats exist in the next 18 months?

Worksheet 9   SWOT Analysis

	OPPORTUNITIES	THREATS
STRENGTHS		
WEAKNESSES		

Unique opportunity for the next 6 months:

_____

_____

_____

Challenge to address in the next 6 months:

_____

_____

_____

Worksheet 10

Community Partners and Stakeholders

List all of the organizations, groups, and individuals in each category that are critical to your organization. Consider why they are important to your organization. Place a check in front of those organizations with which your organization might collaborate.

Category/Name	Reason for Connection
Colleagues at other organizations	

_____	_____
_____	_____
_____	_____
_____	_____
_____	_____
_____	_____

Organizations with similar program interests and values or with whom we partner

_____	_____
_____	_____
_____	_____
_____	_____
_____	_____
_____	_____

Organizations that oppose our work

_____	_____
_____	_____
_____	_____
_____	_____
_____	_____
_____	_____

Clients_____

Activists/advocates (for us)_____

Activists/advocates (against us)_____

Board members_____

Volunteers_____

Category/Name	Reason for Connection
Private foundations	
_____	_____
_____	_____
_____	_____
_____	_____
Corporate foundations	
_____	_____
_____	_____
_____	_____
_____	_____
Donors	
_____	_____
_____	_____
_____	_____
_____	_____
Community leaders	
_____	_____
_____	_____
_____	_____
_____	_____
_____	_____
_____	_____
Community groups	
_____	_____
_____	_____
_____	_____
_____	_____
_____	_____
_____	_____
Church groups	
_____	_____
_____	_____
_____	_____
_____	_____

Category/Name	Reason for Connection
Reporters, editors, media outlets, specific programs	
_____	_____
_____	_____
_____	_____
_____	_____
Government officials/policy makers	
_____	_____
_____	_____
_____	_____
_____	_____
Non-government policy makers	
_____	_____
_____	_____
_____	_____
_____	_____
Parents	
_____	_____
_____	_____
_____	_____
Educators/teachers	
_____	_____
_____	_____
_____	_____
Corporations—senior managers	
_____	_____
_____	_____
_____	_____
Small business owners	
_____	_____
_____	_____
_____	_____
_____	_____

Category/Name	Reason for Connection
Youth	

Youth

_____

_____

_____

_____

Healthcare providers

_____

_____

_____

_____

Social service agencies

_____

_____

_____

_____

_____

_____

_____

_____

Review your list and select at least 5 priority audiences that will be the focal point of your strategic communication efforts.

1. _____

2. _____

3. _____

4. _____

5. _____

Step Three: Focusing the Plan
Target Audiences

A nonprofit organization's communications strategy is far more likely to succeed if it considers which audiences it actually has the potential to reach. Nonprofit organizations need to focus their attention on the groups and individuals who are most likely to help them fulfill their missions:

1. *The Active Public:* Those who are already involved with the organization
2. *The Engaged Public:* Those who are already working on the issue
3. *The Aware Public:* Those who already care about the issue and those who could be easily persuaded to become involved in the issue

By focusing strategically on these groups, an organization is much more likely to use its limited resources effectively. The more narrowly an organization defines its audiences and the better it understands them, the more likely it can craft messages that will reach and motivate those audiences to take positive action.

How often has someone said the nonprofit's aim is to reach the "general public" or "we need to do a public education campaign"? The "general public" amounts to more than 6 billion people. Trying to reach all of them is certainly not strategic; nor is it something than most organizations can afford. This is why it is critical not only to identify the organization's target audience(s)—or "publics"—but to learn as much as possible about them in order to be successful in all communications endeavors.

Audiences are formed when people (a) face a similar problem, (b) recognize that a problem exists, and (c) organize to do something about that problem. Within the general public, there are people who are already engaged in working on the issue. They may be members of the nonprofit organization, peer organizations, or constituents who care about the issue. This "activist" audience is the audience more likely to seek out information and most likely to act on that information. It should be the base for the

Exhibit 5.1 Targeting Critical Audiences: Activist Public

nonprofit and its communications activities because it is the place where the organization will have the greatest return on its investment (see Exhibit 5.1).

Beyond this activist audience is an informed audience, the "engaged" audience, people who know about the issue and share some of the concerns of the activist audience. This group may include people who have reason to be affected by the issue but have yet to recognize it, as well as people who are engaged and aware of the issue but who have not yet become involved. The challenge with this audience is to focus their awareness of the problem and to motivate them, to organize their recognition of the problem into action.

With this targeted group, the message strategy must be to transform their awareness of the problem with an urgent call to action, additional information that demonstrates that their active engagement could be the missing factor in achieving significant change. This group may not stay as involved as the activist audience, but its members offer critical support in times when quick actions are desired and additional people power is needed (see Exhibit 5.2).

It is important to keep in mind that regardless of how important the mission is, or how critical the need that an organization addresses, every nonprofit is in competition for attention with a great many worthy issues and causes. Once an organization has succeeded in mobilizing the *activist* and *engaged* audiences, it can address the challenges of reaching those who care but are not involved. After that, there will be time to try to persuade those who ought to be aware but are not. The part of the population directly connected to the organization and its issues presents it with the greatest opportunities for success. Over time, success with the activist and engaged

Exhibit 5.2 Targeting Critical Audiences: Engaged Public

audiences will raise awareness around a growing circle of *engaged* audiences who can then be recruited to become part of the activist and engaged audiences.

Understand Your Audience

As the "Critical Stakeholder" exercise in Chapter 4 demonstrated, most organizations have multiple audiences. Constituents, clients, activists, board members, volunteers, policy makers, and donors are each part of the rich constellation supporting an organization and its mission. The interests of each of these audiences, their level of awareness, and the degree of their commitment will vary. For example, within the donor audience, there are high- and low-dollar donors. They act in different ways financially yet both support the organization and its mission. Likewise, policy makers may care about the organization and its mission, but their responsibilities include commitments to their constituents and to a broader policy agenda. Understanding the motivation of each audience segment enables the organization to develop a tailored approach that speaks directly to the needs and desires of that audience.

Worksheet 11, found at the end of this chapter, can be used to help rank the audiences that are essential to the organization's work.

Although there are occasions when an organization's key audience may be an audience of one—a specific funder, policy maker, or board chair—it is more likely that the organization will need to communicate with many individuals or groups simultaneously. Because resources—funds, staff, and time—are limited, the organization will need to focus on a few key audiences before expanding its effort to other audience groups. This staggered approach makes good use of resources and, at the same time, creates the momentum needed for long-term success.

For example, a nonprofit that cares about the health needs of preschoolers may need to enlist the support of local school boards and principals for an in-school health clinic before it can begin communicating with parents and students about the clinic and why they should support it. If the school board rejects the proposal for the clinics, the nonprofit may need to send a message to parents and students to "Tell the school board you want the clinic." If the clinic gets the go-ahead from the school board, the nonprofit's message may be: "We're happy to announce that your children will have a place to go when they get sick or have an accident at school."

Some organizations and groups may be priority audiences because they have contact with or the ability to influence or reach other audiences that are critical to organizational goals. These "outreach partners" can help an organization reach key audiences, often more cost-effectively than trying to reach those key audience members directly.

For example, instead of mounting an extensive and expensive consumer media campaign, if a clinic wants to provide prenatal care to 50 low-income women each month, it might solicit help from social service agencies, pregnancy testing centers, low-income housing associations, or homeless shelters to reach the women who are most in need of these services.

Consider an organization that has worked hard on healthcare reform. A bill has finally made its way to the governor's desk. The nonprofit may want to examine its high-dollar donor list or board of directors to see who has a connection with the governor. That person might deliver the organization's message to the governor more effectively than the nonprofit's executive director or a small group of volunteers.

The more specific you can be when defining your key audiences and potential outreach partners, the easier it will be to find the most effective ways to communicate with them.

It should be apparent by now that it is not enough simply to identify key audiences. The next step—and the more difficult task—is to learn as much as possible about them, to "stand in their shoes" and relate to their point of view. Ideally, the organization must be able to say that it honestly knows what the people from each audience are like, what makes them tick, what problems and prejudices they have, and what they think and feel about the organization, its issues, and its programs and services. This familiarity will have a positive influence on how the audience experiences the organization, its work, and its efforts to recruit their participation.

All too often, a nonprofit makes assumptions about certain audiences that may or may not be true. In order to use resources most efficiently, the communications action team (CAT) must challenge these assumptions at the outset to set successful objectives, craft more effective messages, and adopt appropriate strategies.

Three types of information are used to segment audiences: demographic, geographic, and psychographic.

Demographic Information

In the United States, the U.S. Census Bureau is the central source for demographic information. These data include everything from unemployment statistics and public health indicators to public transportation and market research. Research has shown that the predictability of various preferences and wants within specific demographic sectors is surprisingly accurate. Demographic factors are a key tool to help understand the perspectives of the target audience.

Each individual experiences certain milestone events—marriage, the birth of a child or children, separation or divorce, the death of a spouse or parent—that mark the beginning and ending of different phases of life but also change the experience of life forever. When certain demographic factors are combined, most notably age, marital status, and presence of children, a picture of a person's life begins to emerge.

For example, a family of four with an income of $50,000 worries about paying the bills; a family of four with an income of $75,000 worries how to save for college education. Occupation shapes our day-to-day experience of the world, and it is affected by economic cycles. Bus drivers spend 8 hours on the road; store clerks spend their shifts behind a counter; construction workers spent their workday outdoors, while lawyers, doctors, and business professionals spent 12 to 15 hours inside buildings. The way we spend our days influences where and how we receive information and colors the choices that we make. Demographics provide important clues that can inform our communications strategies.

Geographic Information

Where people live also provides important clues as to where they receive information and what issues have priority in their lives. Whether someone lives in a rural, suburban, or urban setting influences his or her access to information. The region of the country, the state, and the neighborhoods where people choose to live also influences our understanding of what matters to them.

Psychographic Information

"Psychographics is the use of psychological, sociological, and anthropological factors, such as benefits desired, self-concept and lifestyle to determine how the market is segmented by the propensity of groups within the market—and their reasons—to make a particular decision about a product, person, ideology or otherwise hold an attitude or use a medium."[1] Three basic psychographic categories are how people spend their time, what is important to them in their immediate surroundings, and their opinions about how they view themselves and the world around them.

Consider what these factors could contribute to understanding the key audiences for the organization and its strategic work:

- Activities: work, hobbies, social events, vacations, entertainment, community, sports
- Interests: family, home, job, recreation, fashion, media, achievements
- Opinions: social issues, politics, business, economic, education, culture
- Demographics: age, education, income, occupation, family size, dwelling, stage in the life cycle

Leadership Potential

There is an additional factor, leadership potential that helps to distinguish audiences that are important because of their ability to reach and influence others. These stakeholders will become an important part of the communication strategies. They can serve as spokespeople and support outreach efforts to those groups where they have special connections. When considering these audiences, it is useful to consider these characteristics

- *Covert power:* These are individuals who have the authority to influence decisions in an unexpected or "unofficial" way. In *The Tipping Point*, Malcolm Gladwell refers to these people as Connectors.[2]
- *Position:* These are individual who have power by virtue of status in an organization or in the community: heads of organizations, community

---

[1]Emanual Demby, as quoted in Piirto, Rebecca, *Beyond Mind Games: The Marketing Power of Psychographics* (New York: American Demographic Books, 1991), p. 18.
[2]Gladwell, Malcolm, *The Tipping Point: How Little Things Can Make a Big Difference* (Boston, New York, and London: Little, Brown, and Company, 2002), p. 67.

leaders, and elected officials are examples of people with positional power.

- *Reputation:* These are individuals who are described by others as knowledgeable or influential on a given issue or within a specific community. Teachers, church leaders, and activists are examples of people that community members turn to for direction on issues and community events.
- *Membership:* People who share membership in an organization have power because of their connection to the organization and its work. Partnering with those who have power within these organizations can give added stature to your message and requests for action.

Each of these leadership characteristics can contribute to tailoring the messages and strategies to ensure a better outcome for the strategic communications plan. Individuals with covert power can be recruited to deliver one-on-one messages to people in leadership positions. Individuals with positional power can be asked to speak to the leaders of their organization and to encourage them to join coalitions or to enlist the organization to support community action. Individuals with reputations can be asked to join public forums and to raise their voice in support of initiatives being sponsored by the nonprofit. And, individuals who are members of an organization can be asked to recruit their friends and colleagues to take specific action steps. In each instance, the message and the means for delivering that message will be different.

Profile Each Priority Audience

Consider the audience groups that are top priority for the organization. Use Worksheet 12 to list their habits, interests and activities, shared experiences, cultural attitudes and values, and personal beliefs and opinions. What adjectives describe them? What is important to them in their lives? What motivates them to do what they do? Look at what you already know—or think you know—and write it down. Try to picture a real person—someone you know—who embodies this audience (perhaps an actual member of your target audience). Write her name down as a way to jog your memory when working with this audience. This personal connection to a real person will help you reinforce the idea that the larger audience is really a group of individuals just like "Sheila."

Worksheet 12, found at the end of this chapter, can be used to profile the audience.

Research Your Audience

Many times, designing the audience profile reveals that the organization does not know its priority audiences as well as it should. Research can help the CAT make informed decisions rather than simply guessing the answers. Research can help the CAT fill in the blanks and design strategies that can more effectively reflect the needs and interests of each audience. Some are expensive, such as market research studies or polling reports. Other methods are more affordable and can easily be completed with a simple investment of some staff or volunteer time. Carefully define the information that is needed and how that information is connected to the desired project outcomes.

Some of these resources are readily available in your home or office. Keep in mind that some techniques may be more appropriate if the target audience is *individuals*. Other tools may be more useful for understanding *organizations* and potential partnerships.

Media Review

Routinely, members of the CAT should observe and read everything it can that relates to the organization: books, government reports, academic studies, analyses of census data, periodicals, and online information. Monitor online discussion groups that focus on topics of interest to the organization. Watch for trends. Pay attention to polling conducted by local or national media. Take time to do online searches—use the audience group category as a keyword for the search.

Readership Surveys or Membership Questionnaires

Many organizations conduct written surveys of newsletter readers or as part of a direct mail piece. In surveying:

1. Choose a representative sample of the audience to receive the survey.
2. Develop clear questions.
3. Follow up to help produce a meaningful response rate.

Piggyback Surveys

Several national research organizations regularly conduct omnibus surveys that combine questions from a number of sponsors. Look into the possibility of adding a few questions to these surveys. This can be a cost-effective way to get information from a national or regional sample.

Exit Interviews or Evaluation Surveys

Sometimes the best way to find out what a target audience is thinking or why its members do what they do is to simply ask them. When people call the organization, ask them how they heard about it. When the organization conducts a workshop, hosts a forum, or convenes a coalition meeting, circulate a quick evaluation questionnaire before letting people leave.

Informal Discussions

Many organizations bring together representatives from key audience groups to engage in an informal conversation about issues or services. These informal discussions may be useful in gleaning the attitudes of these particular audience members; be mindful, though, that the opinions expressed by these individuals may not necessarily translate to a larger audience.

One of the benefits of the informal conversation is that you can elicit responses from several people at once and test their saliency against other arguments that have also been introduced into the discussion. One of the drawbacks is that the opinions of one or two may influence others unduly.

Focus Groups

The success of a focus group depends on the design of the questions, the skill and training of the moderator, the careful selection of the panelists, and the correct interpretation of the resulting conversation. With proper preparation, staff members can convene focus groups of constituents who know the organization. For focus groups with those outside of the organization's circle, it is probably best to work with a professional facilitator.

Rules of the Road: Targeting Your Audience

1. The CAT must carefully consider which segments of the target audiences are most connected to the organization's mission and issues. Do not try to reach the "general public."
2. The CAT will establish priorities among the audiences and consider each of the key audiences separately.
3. The CAT will cluster audiences according to their values, connection to the organization, and the desired action.
4. As it does its work, the CAT should:
   - Remember that many issues and causes compete for the attention of the audience. Knowing what is important to the key audiences will help the organization understand why the audience cares about its mission, issues, and programs.
   - Remember to consider and target secondary audiences or "outreach partners" who may be influential with key audiences. These power players can also be important audiences for implementing the plan.
   - Never take the audience for granted, no matter how well the staff feels that it knows them.

Remember:

Strategic communications puts the audience first.

Worksheet 11   Audience Identification

Step 1. Review the list below and rate each "audience" in terms of its importance to your work (somewhat important, critically important or not applicable).

Step 2. Decide whether you have been effective or not effective at reaching out to them.

Step 3. Rank the 5 most critical audiences for this planning process. Check the appropriate boxes.

Category	Step 1				Step 2		Step 3
	N/A	Somewhat Important	Important	Critical	Not Effective	Effective	Rank the Top 5
					1 2 3	4 5	
					1 2 3	4 5	
					1 2 3	4 5	
					1 2 3	4 5	
					1 2 3	4 5	
					1 2 3	4 5	
					1 2 3	4 5	
					1 2 3	4 5	
					1 2 3	4 5	
					1 2 3	4 5	

Worksheet 12   Audience Profile

Audience _____

1. Describe your audience: What are their concerns? What characteristics of your audience are important to your organization (e.g., their education levels, income levels; family size, health issues)?

2. Why are they important to you?

3. Why should your audience care about your organization and its issues?

4. What do you want from this audience?

5. How does this audience receive information?

6. Are there particular individuals who have credibility or power over the target audience? What are their names?

7. Are there other individuals that can help you better reach this target audience? Who?

8. How will you know if you have successfully reached this audience?

TIPS: Don't assume that you know the audience, even if you have worked with them for a while. Put yourself in their shoes and think about what they need and want from your organization. Remember, the general public is not an audience.

CHAPTER

Step Four: Fostering Audience Support Communications Objectives

The strategic communications plan is the action plan that supports the organization's strategic plan. Goals are outcome statements that guide the organization as a whole, including programs, administration, finance, and governance functions. In addition, each department or program will have goals for its own individual purposes within the organization. Each goal will have two or more specific objectives.

An objective is a precise, measurable result that contributes to the achievement of the goal. Objectives can be either *process objectives* or *outcome objectives*. *Process objectives* describe activities that will be undertaken by the organization. *Outcome objectives* describe the results that the organization seeks to achieve with the people that it serves. If the objective describes something that the communications action team (CAT), senior management, other staff, or volunteers will undertake, it is most likely an activity or process objective. If the objective describes a change in behavior, skills, or awareness of external audiences, clients, or service customers, it is most likely an outcome objective.[1]

Communications objectives are the objectives that help the organization achieve its program objectives. They describe who needs to be reached and what change is desired and sets a time frame for achieving the desired result. Communications objectives help set up the framework for message development and the strategies for disseminating the message.

---

[1]Michael Allison and Jude Kaye, *Strategic Planning for Nonprofit Organizations* (Hoboken, NJ: John Wiley & Sons, 2005), pp. 237–239.

The following terms are used in the development of communications objectives:

Project goals	What does the organization want to make happen?
Process objectives—action the organization takes	How does the organization intend to make it happen?
Outcome objectives—results that the organization seeks to achieve with the people it serves?	What does the organization want others to do?
Communications objectives—action the organization needs from others	Who needs to be reached, what results are desired, and how and when will that happen?

Measurable objectives provide the benchmarks that will be used to evaluate the effectiveness of each effort and to ensure movement toward eventually achieving each project goal. Measurable objectives lie at the heart of an organization's program strategies and project activities. These objectives also will be used to formulate communications objectives from which the communications plan will emerge.

All measurable objectives should include a realistic target date. Objectives should state the number of people or percentage of audience to be reached to establish a measure to evaluate success. If money can be used as a measurement, determine the amount, stated in dollars or as a percentage of a current benchmark, to be reached. Objectives should state exactly what the organization hopes to accomplish with the people reached or the money raised.

Unlike program goals, program and communications objectives are limited in scope and often evolve or change over time. When an objective is met, it often leads to the development of additional objectives until the overall program goal is achieved. Frequently, program and communications objectives build on prior work of earlier objectives, generating momentum toward the achievement of the overall program goal.

The key to creating effective measurable objectives is to be as specific as possible.

An example of an objective without measurements might be

Create awareness within the community of the effects of alcohol on youth.

To turn this into a measurable objective, indicate the targeted audience, area of change, direction of the change, degree of change desired, and time frame or target date. It may be helpful to include a definition of who is to be educated, the number of individuals needed to claim success, and the target date to complete this objective.

The example can be restated as a measurable outcome objective:

Ensure that all parents in School District 20 understand how alcohol affects the learning capacity, self-esteem, and health of our youth by convincing 50 parents to become involved in Parents Fight Back by July.

What measurements are used to clarify and qualify this objective?

Target audience	Parents in School District 20
Area of change	Parents understand the effects of alcoholism on youth
Direction of change	Increase awareness
Degree of change	All parents informed and 50 parents become active in ''Parents Fight Back''
Time frame/target date	July 1

In this case, the objective is focused on the outcome of educating all parents and recruiting 50 parents to participate in the Parents Fight Back event in July.

The example can also be restated as a measurable process objective:

Develop educational materials and host a forum to recruit parents for the Parents Fight Back event in July.

Target audience	Staff
Area of change	Develop materials; host forum
Direction of change	Recruit parent participation
Degree of change	Materials sent to all parents Host forum on ''Parents Fight Back''
Time frame/target date	May–June

In this case, the organization is responsible for implementing the process. Its activities must occur prior to the actual event date in July to be successful. Staff members must implement strategies to ensure that the appropriate materials are developed and disseminated and that strategies are initiated (phone call, parent-to-parent outreach, etc.) to guarantee that the recruitment objective is met.

The objective becomes a communications objective when the process objective and the outcome objective are linked through the communications function.

Inform all parents about the effects of alcohol on youth.

Recruit 50 parents to participate in "Parents Fight Back."

Target audience	Parents in School District 20
Area of change	Parents participate in the program
Direction of change	Parents take action
Degree of change	50 parents become active in "Parents Fight Back"
Time frame/target date	July 1

With specific benchmarks in place, it is possible to develop appropriate strategies and programs to achieve the objective and to measure progress. The communications objective clarifies who the target audience will be and what the message challenge is and suggests the appropriate vehicles and strategies for achieving the objective. In this instance, parents will need information about the impact of alcohol on youth and promotional materials about the group being created. They will also need clear messages about how they, as parents, can make a difference. A subsequent communications objective will mobilize parents to educate other parents and/or initiate conversations with their children.

The SMART Test

Clearly articulated goals and objectives that can be monitored actively will ensure the success of the communications plan. Evaluating whether the organization is close to the targets it has set provides critical information that can be used to fine-tune and refocus communications efforts, when necessary.

For each objective, the CAT should apply the SMART test: Is the objective Specific, Measurable, Achievable, Realistic and Time-bound?

Specific objectives identify the target audience, the direction of change, the area of change, the target population, and the time frame for achieving the objective. These elements set up the parameters for *measurable* objectives and help the CAT determine whether the objective has been met. *Achievable* means that the objective is possible. For the previous example, this means that 50 parents can be recruited. If the total pool of parents is 100, recruiting half of them may be possible. If the total pool of parents is 50, however, recruiting 100% participation may be achievable, but it may not be realistic. *Realistic* means that the objective is doable. In other words, in the desired time frame, the organization can do the necessary work (develop the materials, disseminate the materials, recruit parent participants, plan the forum and execute the event in July). The *time* frame (July) ensures that all the steps will be completed and provides a benchmark for measuring whether the objective was achieved or not.

Rules of the Road: Developing Measurable Objectives

1. The CAT should review the strategic plan and identify the goals, process, and outcome objectives for each one.
2. The CAT should identify the target audiences it wants to involve in change.
3. The CAT should be specific about what must be accomplished and set specific targets—either in numbers or percentages of an existing figure—that can be counted and/or measured along the way.
4. The CAT is responsible for ensuring that the objectives can be monitored and measured. It must consider what needs to occur and what evidence must exist in order to know that the objective has been met.
5. The CAT must also set realistic time frames to ensure that the work gets done to accomplish the objective.

Cycle of the Communications Process

When developing the communications objectives, it is helpful to consider the cycle of communications. First, people become informed about an interest or cause, then they become interested or engaged and want to know more. At that point, they actually may become motivated to participate or take action in some way. Once they are active participants, it will be possible to keep them engaged through additional activities or opportunities that enable them to stay involved.

As Exhibit 6.1 demonstrates, each quadrant builds on the one before. Once the organization takes action to inform an audience, it can begin to engage the individual in a discussion and initiate a relationship. At this point

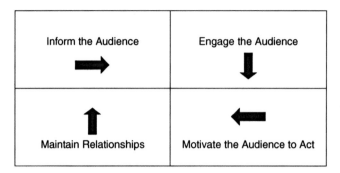

Exhibit 6.1   Communications Process Cycle

of engagement, the individual has indicated interest and asked for more information. With an appropriate set of opportunities for action, the person likely will be motivated to act. The final stage in the communications process is maintaining and strengthening the relationship, providing new opportunities for engagement. Completing the final stage can lead back to the beginning of the cycle—informing the audience of related issues or initiating involvement in a new round of activities.

Create the Communications Objectives

Process objectives focus on the tasks required to meet a program goal. The communications objective focuses on audience members and what must be done to inform and engage them, enlist their support or participation, and/ or maintain their level of involvement. A communications objective includes measures similar to a project objective but communications objectives require action by the organization in order to elicit a desired action from the target audience.

Communications objectives:

- Identify the target audience.
- Define the desired nature or direction of the change.
- Identify the change to occur (i.e., the specific knowledge, attitude, or behavior to be achieved).
- Determine the degree or amount of change desired.
- Establish a target date.

One way to build strong communications objectives is to consider the verbs of the sentences. The verbs in communications objectives describe the action that will be taken by the organization—usually a communications activity—and suggest the desired change that will occur in the audience.

Verbs that Indicate a Communications Objective

Build consensus	Mobilize
Conduct	Promote
Discuss	Provide
Educate	Sign up, register
Enlist support	Teach
Inform	

Like a program objective, each communications objective will identify at least one audience group. Although a communications objective often has several audiences, it may be easier to establish a separate communications objective for each audience.

Communications objectives often are differentiated by the nature of the intended change and the specific knowledge, attitude, or behavior to be achieved. For example, the first level of communication is simply to inform someone about a topic. Educating someone about the same topic or issue takes more effort but may produce a more active or committed audience member. Mobilizing people to do something (e.g., change a certain behavior, support your organization, contribute funds) builds on the success of your engagement with this audience.

The final step is maintaining the relationships by creating new opportunities for each audience to be actively engaged.

Communications Objectives: Some Examples Using the Cycle of Communications

Example 1: Create Awareness. Promote our scholarship program by presenting an orientation about our organization at the April Chamber of Commerce breakfast to recruit at least five corporate sponsors.

Target audience	Business community
Specific area of change	Business community becomes aware of us
Nature of change	Promote awareness of our work
Amount of change	Identify 15 potential corporate sponsors
Time frame	By May

Example 2: Engage the Audience.   Enlist support by holding one-on-one meetings during the summer with each of the 15 potential corporate sponsors. Present the criteria for being a corporate sponsor and invite participation. Conduct follow-up meetings and calls as appropriate to reach recruitment goals.

Target audience	15 potential corporate sponsors
Specific area of change	Engage in discussion about corporate sponsorship
Nature of change	Business becomes interested in our work
Amount of change	One-third (5) agree to become sponsors
Time frame	By August

Example 3: Motivate to Act.   Convince five businesses to become corporate sponsors by fall.

Target audience	15 potential business sponsors
Specific area of change	5 commit to become sponsors
Nature of change	Become sponsors
Amount of change	Financial contribution and designate a business representative for the kick-off event
Time frame	By September

Example 4: Maintain Relationships.   Share program updates on student performance, invite their participation in the year-end assembly, give recognition in our annual report, and invite them to recruit other business leaders to become sponsors for the second year of the program.

Target audience	5 business sponsors
Specific area of change	Share program data
Nature of change	Invite participation
Amount of change	Sponsors become ambassadors of our program
Time frame	End of school year

Worksheet 13 walks you through the process of developing communications objectives. Specify the target audience and the desired action, indicate the size of the audience and the number or percentage that needs to take action. Break down the audience members by where they fall in the cycle of communications: how many need to be informed, how many are ready to be engaged, how many may be motivated to act, and how many are already active and need to be encouraged to take additional action to maintain the relationship. Use action verbs to indicate the impact objectives that you desire from the audience by specifying the nature of the desired change: what you want each segment to do. Also use action verbs to indicate the process objectives the organization must take (e.g., educate, teach, inform, provide, conduct, enlist, mobilize, discuss, promote, build consensus). Finally, apply the SMART test. Is this objective Specific, Measurable, Achievable, Realistic, and Time-bound? Complete communications objectives for each of your priority audiences.

 Worksheet 13, found at the end of this chapter, facilitates the process of developing communications objectives.

Rules of the Road: Tips for Developing Communications Objectives

1. The CAT should build communications objectives for each program goal tailored to every priority target audience. The communications objectives can be either process objectives (staff initiated) or impact objectives (audience initiated).
2. The CAT then considers the target audience, the area of change that the organization wants to occur, and the strategy for achieving this change with the audience. It will need to develop communications objectives that educate, inform, promote, or build/maintain relationships.
3. As the CAT thinks about the reasons it is communicating with different people or groups, it considers what the organization hopes to achieve with each target audience. Doing this sets up the framework for message development.
4. As much as possible the CAT should clarify the nature of the desired change and the specific knowledge, attitude, or behavior to be achieved.

Worksheet 13   Develop SMART Communications Objectives

Remember that communications objectives focus on the cycle of the communications process (to inform, engage, motivate to act, and maintain relationships). Specify the nature of the desired change. Communications objectives have action verbs (e.g., educate, teach, inform, provide, conduct, enlist, mobilize, discuss, promote, build consensus). Communications objectives provide the standard for measuring success. Start by indicating the size of the audience and the percentage that needs to take action.

Communications Objective #1

Target Audience: _____

Number: _____

Select One: ☐ Inform   ☐ Engage   ☐ Motivate   ☐ Maintain

Desired Action: _____

_____

Target Date: _____

State Objective: _____

_____

_____

Communications Objective #2

Target Audience: _____

Number: _____

Select One: ☐ Inform   ☐ Engage   ☐ Motivate   ☐ Maintain

Desired Action: _____

_____

Target Date: _____

State Objective: _____

_____

_____

Apply the SMART test. Are the communications objectives Specific, Measurable, Achievable, Realistic and Time-Bound?

7

Step Five: Promoting the Nonprofit Organization Issue Frames and Message Development

The organization's goals and objectives are the foundation of the communications plan, but the message is the heart of its efforts to reach target audiences. Message development is more art than science. Audience research can help identify an audience's trigger points—what will be influential, what will fall flat, what is likely to conjure up a negative response—but understanding the power of language, imagery, and motivation are essential to effective messaging.

Many of us confuse messages with sound bites, taglines, slogans, or statements about the organization. A message may reflect these things—or occasionally incorporate them—but an *effective* message is something much more fundamental and substantive. A message comprises two or three sentences and communicates a complete thought. Indeed, the message is what inspires and anchors sound bites, slogans and tag lines.

Message development is a process that includes several steps. To set the context, here are a few definitions that we will use in describing the process:

Image: The personal traits and attributes that convey the impression of the organization, its leadership, and its purpose.

Mission statement: One to several paragraphs that incorporates an organization's goals, values, and ideals. Because this statement is used in fundraising appeals and annual reports, it is often written in formal language.

Organization description: A 20- to 25-word statement that uses spoken language to convey what the organization does and how it makes a difference. This description becomes the platform most people use to understand the organization and the work that it does. It is often referred to as the elevator speech, the opening sentence that you use to inform people about the organization.

Message: A limited body of information that is used consistently by an organization to offer reasons for an audience to act on the organization's behalf. Messages help an organization convey why it does what it does, why it matters, and why an audience should care about its work. Messages convey who the nonprofit is and what it does and persuades others to adopt the nonprofit's point of view. Messages are critical to the success of the organization and its agenda. Effective, persuasive messages should clearly define the issue, connect it to the target audience, and indicate a course of action. A strong message will help the nonprofit organization achieve its objectives—whether that means changing public policy, recruiting volunteers, or getting people to change specific behaviors.

Slogan/tagline: A short phrase or sentence that highlights the message. A slogan is not a message but rather a memorable phrase that can reinforce the message, such as the Peace Corps' *Toughest Job You'll Ever Love,* or the Army's *Be All That You Can Be.* Slogans are not necessarily complete sentences, nor do they necessarily describe an organization. Instead, they are memorable, short, and snappy. Using the mission statement described earlier, an example of a slogan for the Logan County Volunteer Center might be *Volunteers Make Connections.*

Message platform: Includes the mission, vision, and values statements, the brief organization description, slogans/taglines, a one-page fact sheet about the organization and its history, any other promotional materials about the organization's essential programs and services, and the persuasive messages developed for each target audience. The message platform serves as the organization's language toolkit.

Message framing: A process used to analyze the values, perceptions, and personal connections that people bring to an issue. The term refers both to the way the public views issues and the values and assumptions that reinforce those views. Therefore, framing can be discussed in terms of both the external environment—the general social and cultural understandings in which audiences tend to assign meaning to issues—and how the organization tries to shape, define, or package information to change an audience's viewpoint or to correspond with the way an audience approaches an issue.

The message development process is not linear, and there is no one right way to develop effective messages. The four key steps in the process for the communications action team (CAT) are:

1. Identify three or four key themes.
2. Decide on the message frame.
3. Create an overall organization description or "umbrella message" for the organization.
4. Develop persuasive messages targeted to the priority audiences using the message triangle. The message triangle focuses on three components: the issue, why it matters to the audience and the desired ask, or request to take action.

The essence of a message is based on how the people involved in the organization think and feel about the issue, program, or some specific concern as well as how the organization would like the solution to be discussed. The most successful messages are expressed in ways that resonate with the perspectives, experiences, and values of the target audience. (Remember: Often this is not the same as *your* perception of a target audience's values, opinions, attitudes, or beliefs.)

Good messages balance the organization's values, goals, and objectives with the beliefs, attitudes, and opinions of the target audience. If the problem and the solution are defined within the framework of the audience's perspective and values, it is much more likely that the audience will listen to the message and agree with how the issue has been framed—the first step in getting people to think about and possibly actively support the solution that the organization is suggesting.

In developing messages, it is important to know who needs to be reached (e.g., local business leaders, volunteers, elderly people, and legislators). Although it may not be necessary to create entirely new messages for each audience, messages will work much better if they are tweaked to target specific kinds of people. In fact, messages that work in concert with each other have the potential for building a critical mass of support across a range of audiences and supporters.

Define the Key Themes

Every organization needs more than a single message for its issues or programs. Ideally, the CAT should identify three or four key themes that will be the foundation for the messages that anyone can use to talk about the organization, its programs, and its issue. These themes provide the emotional grist that best responds to challenges, arguments, or questions that may arise for the organization. The themes can then be mixed and matched, creating messages that reinforce each other and reinforce how the organization defines a problem and its solution.

For example, the key themes of Caring Connection are helping individuals and families making informed decisions about end-of-life care; the importance of talking with health professionals, clergy, and family member about preferences for treatment; and encouraging communities to actively support these discussions.

The themes for Planet 3000 include pursuing research to support an eco-human systems approach, promoting individual change to reduce the global impact of humans, and advocating for policies to protect the environment and ensure positive citizen behaviors.

The CAT is responsible for reviewing the vision, goals, and mission statement and identifying the three or four themes that will ground the organization's work for the next three to five years. The next step is to understand how the general public understands those themes and whether and how the issues are being discussed in the media and other public discourse.

Message Frames

Each nonprofit has a view about how it would like the public to understand and relate to its mission, its programs, and its issues, but in most instances, the general public and the aware public are much more likely to have their understanding of the issues shaped by the media, their daily experiences, and other external forces. George Lakoff, a professor of linguistics and cognitive science at the University of California, Berkeley, describes frames as "mental structures that shape the way we see the world."[1]

Frames for Caring Connections include the belief that making decisions about how to approach the end of life before a crisis can provide people and their caregivers peace of mind during a difficult time. The challenge that Caring Connections faces, however, is that many Americans find it difficult to talk about death and would prefer to postpone or avoid making decisions and talking with others about them. The Caring Connections program is based on the tagline: "It's about how you LIVE." LIVE stands for *l*earning about the options; *i*mplementing a plan to honor your desired treatment options; *v*oicing your preferences to family, physicians, and others; and *e*ngaging in community efforts to raise awareness of the LIVE campaign.

Planet 3000 faces a similar challenge. Media framing of environmental challenges often focuses on global perspectives that place responsibility somewhere beyond meaningful personal action and highlights the conflicting policies somewhere in the international arena. To counter this, Planet 3000 has developed frames suggesting that communities have a responsibility and an opportunity to improve the life of each citizen by modeling local

---

[1]George Lakoff, *Don't Think of an Elephant! Know Your Values and Frame the Debate* (White River Junction, VT: Chelsea Green Publishing Co., 2004), p. xv.

policies on human ecosystems (the link between smart policies and human actions); the belief that individual action can make a difference; and promoting solid research that has provided answers for sound policy promoted through community and individual action.

As part of its message development process, the CAT should look at how the community at large is discussing the issues and concerns that the organization addresses.

Guiding Questions

- How do people not connected with the cause look at the issues, the people the organization serves, the organizations with which it partners, and the policies that the organization advances?
- Do they see those concerns the same way that the organization does? Are they passionate about them for the same reasons? Or are their concerns different from those of the organization? If so, how can the organization change its messages to address public concerns and connect the community to itself and its work?

By asking these questions and understanding the community's values and concerns, an organization can evaluate the frames that shape public perceptions of the issues and itself and strengthen its message platform.

After completing their review, the CAT may determine that *re*framing is necessary. *Reframing* is the process of selecting pieces of information and organizing them to produce new perspectives in order to generate public engagement—for example, to advance a particular policy option or to ignite renewed interest in programs or services. By telling an organization's story in a more compelling way, reframing can generate new energy and the necessary public will for achieving the goals of the nonprofit.

Media Role in Framing

The media play a significant role in framing issues that are in the public arena. If an organization's issues are part of a local or national agenda, it is easier to raise money, get the attention of policy makers, and attract new supporters, partners, and donors. However, if communications strategies are not developed to reflect the frames used in popular discourse, the organization may fail to connect with the public and lose opportunities to attract the attention that its cause and its members deserve.

Understanding how the media frame social and political issues for print and news coverage will help the organization appreciate the impact of issue framing. In her book *Compassion Fatigue*, Susan Moeller explains that the tension among what is, what we are shown, what action we take, and what we ultimately remember is at the heart of how we understand the news.[2] Because we are exposed to so many crises and disasters, both global and local, we cannot respond to all of them. Therefore, we respond to very few, if any.

The media use a problem-cause-solution model: What is the issue? Who is responsible? What is the solution? Until the public looks at an issue as a problem that must be addressed, it is unlikely that the community will become engaged in any meaningful way.

To get the public's attention, then, an organization must craft a communications strategy that accomplishes five things:

1. Presents the issue in a way that leads the public to understand that there is a problem.
2. Presents the issue in a way that builds a common public understanding of the problem and its causes.
3. Creates consensus around the best solution to the problem that builds public commitment to that solution.
4. Encourages public belief that the solution is doable and can be achieved. (Sometimes this means that there is the political will to make it happen.)
5. Creates a sense that individual action can advance the desired solution.

Many of society's problems—unemployment, poverty, substance abuse, violence—at the center of nonprofit work can be positioned or debated from multiple frames. Sometimes the problems are systemic and require development of a public policy solution. Sometimes the problems relate to individual responsibility, and individuals must take greater responsibility and modify or change their behaviors. At still other times, elected leaders may not see problems as something that requires government action. When the issue is not in the public domain, the organization must rally others in the community to address the situation or to put pressure on policymakers so that they will address the problem.

Sometimes multiple frames influence public understanding at the same time. In these situations, the CAT must design strategies to integrate the frames. Other times, one frame succeeds for a certain period, only to be overtaken by another point of view. And while nonprofit organizations can influence how an issue is framed—especially with key audiences—there will always be forces beyond their control, such as other organizations with

---

[2]Susan D. Moeller, *Compassion Fatigue: How the Media Sell Disease, Famine, War and Death* (New York, Routledge Press, 1999), p. 53.

opposing viewpoints; the economic health of the nation; or the current cultural lens portrayed through the news, film, television, music, books, and online. Understanding how the issue is framed for the public will help the CAT design an effective communications strategy.

Episodic and Thematic Frames

Shanto Iyengar, a professor of political science and communications studies at the University of California, Los Angeles, suggests that framing an issue to get the public's attention requires the public to feel some relationship to the issue as a problem that can be solved. As long as the media reports on a story in an *episodic* way (today there was another car accident caused by a drunken driver), the public shakes its head but does not feel motivated to take action. However, once the story is presented in a *thematic* way (people who drink and drive cause traffic accidents and traffic fatalities), there is a problem that must have a solution. Episodic frames focus on separate events or particular cases that involve individuals in specific places at specific times. Thematic frames place public issues in a broader context by focusing on general conditions or outcomes. Mothers Against Drunk Driving (MADD) has successfully advocated for state policies against those who drink and drive by instituting campaigns that highlight the responsibility of the drunk driver.

Iyengar concludes that "episodic framing tends to elicit an individual response rather than focusing on societal attributions of responsibility, while thematic framing has the opposite effect."[3] In order to generate community action, an issue must move from an episodic frame to a thematic frame. Once this shift occurs, members of the public see a problem that must be resolved, they expect action to be taken, and they can then be motivated to become involved. The challenge to the nonprofit organization is to discover ways to frame the issues in a thematic context that invites the community to join in pursuing the solution.

Conducting a Framing Analysis

Sometimes a cursory review of media frames is not enough to help an organization recognize how the community responds to its issues. In these instances, it may be helpful to consider conducting a more systematic analysis of all media coverage of the issue.

A framing analysis involves assessing, mapping, and analyzing how the media portray an issue through news coverage. Media frames include the

---

[3]Shanto Iyengar, *Is Anyone Responsible? How Television Frames Political Issues* (Chicago: University of Chicago Press, 1991).

images, opinions, examples, and human faces used to present information. The frame provides a structure that shapes the news story. The analyst examines the items included in the story as well as materials that are left out. A framing analysis is an important tool for an organization that is seeking to understand how its issues are perceived and to examine the relative success of opposing points of view. In conducting a framing analysis, the nonprofit reviews public discussion about an issue, examines arguments on both sides, and assesses the range of arguments and images used to describe the issue.

A framing analysis involves a four-step process:

1. *Task One:* The analyst collects a sample of articles on the issue, and reviews the media sources and viewpoints that represent the range of arguments on it.
2. *Task Two:* The analyst examines the texture of the article by identifying the images and opinions that are used to frame it. Who is quoted? What sources of information are mentioned? What words and images are presented? What arguments are being used? Are there any common catchphrases? The analyst should highlight what is identified as the cause of the problem and who or what is charged with the solution.
3. *Task Three:* The analyst then restates and summarizes the narrative findings into seven categories:
   a. Core position
   b. Catchphrases
   c. Visual images
   d. Source of the problem
   e. Solution to the problem
   f. Predicted outcome
   g. Core principles
4. *Task Four:* The analyst determines what is *not* being said and what examples, arguments, and positions are not represented. This knowledge comes from reviewing other topics on the same issue and the analyst's own knowledge of the issue and research on the perspectives of those involved with the issue.

Among the questions the analyst should consider during the framing analysis are these:

- How is the problem being defined?
- What solutions, if any, are being advanced?
- Who is identified as being responsible for creating the problem?

- Is there a connection among individual, public policy, and community responses to the problem?
- Is it presented as an episodic or a systemic problem?
- Who is held accountable for solving the problem?

Once the organization has analyzed how the issue is being framed in public discourse, it can examine where it and its messages fit into the overall external, or public, frame. If its position is not being well represented in the public debate, the organization can launch a media strategy to bring more focus to its position. If competitors or opponents are doing a better job of presenting their messages to the public, or if the organization finds that its message is inconsistent with the public frame, it may want to reexamine how it discusses the issue or the problem. An organization can change the way it shapes and discusses issues more readily than it can change the meanings and perceptions the public currently ties to those issues. Small nonprofits probably cannot change the national framework surrounding their issue, but they can understand the external frames and reposition their work and messages (without changing their mission and goals) in a way that resonates public understanding.

On an ongoing basis, the CAT should engage the communications audit team, senior management, and the board to act as the eyes and ears of the community, to ensure that the organization is pursuing strategies that fit the community's current information needs and that the issues are framed in a way that builds on those perceptions.

Worksheet 14 guides the communications audit team and/or the CAT to evaluate how the organization, other competing organizations, and the national media present the issues of concern. If there is consensus among the groups that this is an adequate representation, the CAT may move on to Chapter 8. If, however, there is a lack of consensus or a need for a more thorough review of media coverage, use Worksheet 15, which is set up to be used for each relevant piece of media coverage, either print or electronic. Use the worksheet as many times as necessary and then conduct the analysis outlined earlier. You can summarize the analysis on Worksheet 14 or develop a separate framing analysis report.

Worksheet 14, found at the end of this chapter, can be used to help perform a simple framing analysis of the organization.

Worksheet 15, found at the end of this chapter, can be used for each individual media analysis.

Rules of the Road: Conducting a Framing Analysis

1. The analyst should involve senior leadership and/or the board in a discussion of their concerns about how the organization's issues are being discussed among the public. The board and senior staff may also provide insights on ways that the organization could frame or reframe messages. A possible discussion guide could include these questions:

    a. How is the general public discussing our issue?

    b. Do our existing frames continue to work, or have they outlived their usefulness?

    c. Has the perception of our issue evolved over time?

    d. Are our policies and programs still supported by our frames, or have we evolved into new policies and programs without examining the ability of our frames to deliver community support for our work?

2. The analyst should schedule time with the CAT to discuss how the media influences the organization's work. Together they should explore new issues and current events that shape the community's values and perceptions of the organization. The initial framing analysis on particular issues can stimulate these discussions and may help identify new communications opportunities for the organization.

3. The CAT should monitor how the media covers the issues of importance to the organization. It should also train others to listen to outside perspectives, watch television, and listen to programs watched by the audiences the organization tries to reach.

4. The CAT should encourage the staff to use the framing analysis model when presenting its communications recommendations to the full board. It will be helpful to test the various frames with board members since they serve as representatives of the community. They may agree with the interpretation and/or provide additional perspectives that will enrich the analysis.

Reframing

Reframing may become necessary when an organization has lost connection with its supporters; when it wants to reach new audiences; when the political climate has changed and the usual messages no longer resonate; or just to ensure that an organization is reaching its maximum potential. To be successful, reframing must be done in the context of how the public already relates to the facts and the issues involved. An individual organization can reframe its position, but reframing how the public responds requires broader communications strategies beyond the scope of most nonprofit organizations.

The CAT can recommend that a reframing be undertaken as part of the development of the strategic communications plan. It can undertake the work itself or delegate it to others. Because setting aside an organization's values and institutional history and approaching reframing impartially can be very difficult, an outside consultant or communications experts may be needed to help the nonprofit develop a new frame.

There are five basic steps for reframing:

Task 1. Review or conduct public opinion research to understand how the public thinks about a particular social or political issue.

Task 2. Conduct a framing analysis to understand how the media frames the issue in editorials, news stories, and feature publications.

Task 3. Review the research and analysis to understand how the public and media frames influence public choices about the issue.

Task 4. Consider alternative frames to identify other ways of thinking that could encourage people to look at the issue differently.

Task 5. Based on the findings of the framing analysis, the board and staff then (perhaps with the assistance of consultants) can accomplish these tasks:

- Simplify unnecessarily complex issues.
- Set the record straight if there is misleading or suppressed information.
- Forge linkages if there are apparent discontinuities.
- Find new angles to remove or circumvent any barriers to action that exist.

Reframing: Underage Drinking

The issue of underage drinking on college campuses offers a good example of how reframing can affect public commitment and action. In many college towns, drinking on campus is regarded as a rite of passage to adulthood. Tailgate parties, fraternity and sorority parties, pledge events, and drinking games are accepted as rituals that are associated with living on campus. However, studies show that four out of five college students drink alcohol. Two out of five report binge drinking (defined as five or more drinks for men and four or more for women in one sitting). One in five students report three or more binge episodes over a two-week period. Traditional media coverage of underage drinking has been episodic in its framing, usually appearing in early fall during pledge activities and during spring break. In the mid-1990s, health officials, campuses, and communities began to address the issue of alcohol consumption among college students. Extensive studies were conducted on the impact of alcohol on school performance, social interactions, and students' health. The term *binge drinking* was given a precise medical definition that was systematically presented to the media. New approaches were developed for addressing the issue, including talking points that were widely disseminated in college communities. This information reframed the issue by focusing on the true consequences of alcohol abuse. Among the sample talking points were these:

- Alcohol abuse is now a widespread problem on the nation's college campuses that puts students at risk for car accidents, date rape, and academic, medical, and legal problems. In the long run, it may establish a pattern of drinking that can lead to alcoholism and serious health problems.
- Studies show that alcohol is a factor in 66% of student suicides and 60% of all sexually transmitted diseases, including HIV. In addition, one out of four student deaths is related to alcohol use.
- Many students who drink heavily have problems keeping up with their schoolwork and often skip class. Studies show that 41% of all academic problems stem from alcohol abuse, and 28% of the students who drop out of school may do so because of alcohol.

Advocates for alcohol policies were able to change the frame to emphasize a systemic problem that placed responsibility with the individual student, the college administration, and the overall social norms that encouraged drinking. Within this new frame, advocates were able to change the way binge drinking was perceived on campuses and implement policies to discourage such behavior. At campuses across the country, students joined together and made the decision to stay sober. Many colleges and universities implemented strong alcohol policies to keep drinking to a minimum. Some designated alcohol-free dorms and made alcohol-free social events a high priority.

Message Development

First Impressions

What are the first words that your audience—whoever the audience is—hears from you? Probably the name of the organization and what it does. So the way that the organization describes itself is its first impression, and you only get one chance to make a good first impression. In many social situations, first appearances are critical. One Midwestern employer has said that she can tell whether she will hire a job applicant within the first five seconds of meeting a candidate. The same principle applies with an organization description. The audience—whether it is one person or one hundred—may base feelings about the organization on the few sentences used by the receptionist, board members, or others in the community. First impressions are worth their weight in gold.

And yet most organizations have not addressed this need to have strong and consistent messages about the organization and its work. For example, the receptionist may describe the organization very differently than a board member or the chief executive. The head of advocacy may describe the organization much differently than the programs officer. A nonprofit that fails to be consistent loses opportunities to generate a clear and positive image with new contacts.

The first message challenge for the CAT is to determine what the best description should be for the organization: How should the nonprofit be described? Can it be done effectively in fewer than 20 words? How can the organization use words that are easy to understand and prompt the listener to say "Tell me more"?

> Logan County Volunteer Center strives to encourage men, women, and children to get connected to their communities as volunteers. Knowing that large numbers of people in Logan County are willing to volunteer their time to help others, and knowing that the need for such volunteers exists, we work to match volunteers with those in need of them. The Center also provides volunteer trainings, holds annual volunteer recruitment fairs, and works to publicize and honor those volunteers whose commitment improves the community.

The words that the organization uses in relation to its work, its programs, or itself are of critical importance to every audience. One word has the power to offend, to enlighten, or to disgust. Words are not static. They can change in meaning and nuance over time. *Recycling, binge,* and *gay* are all words whose meanings have evolved or changed over time. Nonprofits must evaluate the impact of the words they use with priority audiences to ensure that they still mean what the organization wants them to mean.

Organization Descriptions

Many organizations use their mission statements to describe themselves. However, the mission statement, which is often steeped in history, values, and formal tradition, may not translate well into the spoken word. Other times, in the absence of an organization description, board members, staff members, and others may feel compelled to make something up each time they are asked "Where do you work?" Both of these methods can miss a valuable opportunity to be accurate and spark enthusiasm. It is important to develop a 20- to 25-word description for the organization that can be used all the time, by everyone, in a uniform fashion. This is an important step in building a stronger identity for your organization.

Consider this description taken from an actual organization:

> Resources for Child Caring improves the lives of children by strengthening and supporting the people who care for them. Three key values drive our mission: quality, diversity, and accessibility.

If you heard that from a staff member, would it give you a clear understanding of what the organization actually does and how it benefits people within the community? Is it descriptive enough? Would you know whether you could refer a friend there? *Does it fill you with admiration for the organization?*

Different people respond differently to descriptions such as this, and there are no correct answers. But the CAT should challenge itself: How would the organization description at your nonprofit measure up?

Take a few minutes to cast a critical look at how leaders in the organization describe the organization. Look at brochures, print materials, and the annual report. Are the same words used in each instance? Where is there variation? Does this variation help or hinder the work that the organization does?

This is a prime opportunity to bring in other staff, volunteers, and even board members to join in the process. Ask them to consider whether everyone involved with the organization is using the same language. Is it language that was developed 10 years ago when the organization was created? If so, do the words need to be evaluated and changed? The meaning of language can change or lose impact over time. Would other words better describe what the organization is doing now?

Consider the discipline necessary to get someone's attention in an elevator. If there is only time for 20 words with which to grab this person's attention, are you using the very best words? Do they have immediacy? Are they free from jargon (the internal language that staff members probably use every day but that has little meaning to "civilians")? Does the organization rely on acronyms that are unfamiliar to most people?

A final point to remember is that audiences are people first and audiences second. Because of this, they do not receive messages in a vacuum. There are other messages competing with your message—some that reinforce your message, some that may conflict, some that have nothing to do with the messages of the nonprofit but that are part of the communications environment vying for the attention of your audience. It is important that the messages be truthful as well as clear, persuasive, and concise. Language suggests images that will linger with the audience. Some words trigger an emotional response while others convey the need for a more rational approach. Get rid of words that have been overused or that have no emotional punch. The CAT should consider the language used within the organization. Test each word: Does it convey an emotion? Does it have impact? Does it have meaning to "civilians"? Is it persuasive? Does it contain enough information to give a general idea of what the organization does and compel people to say "Tell me more"?

Messages that Resonate

The messages the organization uses to convey who it is and what it does are critical to its success in meeting its mission, advancing its goals, and promoting its programs. In developing these pieces of the message platform, the CAT needs to figure out whom it is that the organization is trying to reach: potential volunteers? potential corporate partners? policy makers? senior citizens? the board? Although the CAT may not need to create entirely new messages for each audience, the chosen messages will work much better if they are tailored to target specific people. For example, if the organization needs to talk with teenage girls, it probably would not use the same language that it would use with policy makers or potential donors.

Messages are the heart of an organization's communications efforts. Messages convey to the audience why you do what you do; why it matters and why it should be important to them; and what they should feel, think, or do about your work. As mentioned earlier, effective messages are mission driven, audience focused, and action oriented. Effective messages are meaty, easy to understand, and persuasive.

Developing persuasive messages that encourage target audiences to work with the nonprofit requires the organization to put itself into the audience's shoes. To be successfully audience focused, the messages must reflect the values and interests of the audience while suggesting specific actions the audience members can take.

As the CAT begins working on message development, it must consider the broad values that embody the character of the group or organization. Remember, in order to help the audience understand what the organization stands for, whom it represents, and what it is attempting to accomplish, it must consider what motivates each audience. To begin developing a persuasive message, consider these questions:

- What impression do I want to leave with the audience?
- What are two facts I want them to remember?

The overall persuasive message can take several paragraphs to explain in a fact sheet or policy statement but for successful communication, state the message in a simple declarative statement.

Message Triangle

The Issue

Why Your
Audience
Should Care

What You Want Your Audience
To Do, Think, or Feel

To help the CAT develop persuasive messages, consider a triangle method of message development. Although each leg of the triangle can stand on its own, the messages work better in concert. The message can begin with any leg of the triangle. You can start, for example, by asking someone to come to a meeting and then explain what the meeting is about and why you think the person would benefit from attending. You can start by saying "I know that you and I are both concerned about the rising use of alcohol by our high school students" and then say: "Future Generations is launching a program with the local PTA that might be of interest to you. Would you consider coming to the next PTA meeting with me?"

The three steps of the process are:

1. *Define the issue.* One leg of the triangle should contain a message that defines the problem or issue. This leg will create a connection between your organization and the targeted audience. It will be most effective if it reflects common values. An example of a defining statement might be: "Because we live in a large rural area, many people in Logan County feel disconnected from their neighbors in the community. It's also hard to know where to get information to support our families."

2. *Specify why your audience should care.* Another leg of the triangle should contain convey why this is important to the audience: "Maybe volunteering would give you a chance to meet other people and play a key role in creating healthier families in our community."

3. *Explain what you want your audience to do, think, or feel.* The third leg of the triangle should ask audience members to make a specific commitment to the issue or commit to a specific action on behalf of the project: "Come to a volunteer fair at Logan Middle School on Thursday night to find out how volunteering can give you an opportunity to make our community a better place for our families."

Now form a complete, persuasive message by combining the three parts:

> People in Logan County have moved here to enjoy living in a rural area. But because the county is so large, people can feel disconnected from the community and the health services that it offers. Volunteering brings people together and can also play a key role in creating healthier families and communities. Come to a volunteer fair at Logan Middle School on Thursday night to find out how volunteering can give you an opportunity to make our community a better place for our families.

These messages define an issue in the community, propose a solution, and outline a specific action that people can take to address the need.

Building a Message Platform for the Organization

The message platform serves as the organization's language toolkit. It includes the mission, vision, and values statements, the brief organization description, slogans/taglines, a one-page fact sheet about the organization and its history, any other promotional materials about the organization's programs and services, and the persuasive messages developed for each target audience.

Worksheets 16 to 19 are designed to help the CAT understand the current language that the organization uses to describe its work and to identify new words and messages, including the 20- to 25-word organization description, persuasive messages for priority target audiences, and stories that key spokespersons can use to put the human face on the work of the organization.

Worksheet 16, found at the end of this chapter, can be used to help develop descriptive language about the organization.

Worksheet 17, found at the end of this chapter, can be used to create a new organizational description.

Worksheet 18, found at the end of this chapter, can be used to help develop a persuasive message.

Worksheet 19, found at the end of this chapter, can be used to put a human face on the work.

Rules of the Road: Creating Persuasive Messages

1. Remember, the CAT needs to build effective messages that:
   - Reflect the values, practices, personal traits, and policy attitudes of the organization.
   - Deal with the significant concerns of the targeted audience.
   - Is expressed in terms that relate to the day-to-day environment of the audience.
   - Is constantly reinforced and delivered through all the visual, written, and spoken expressions of the organization.
2. The CAT must be disciplined. Keep messages short. Each message should be no longer than three sentences of 10 to 15 words each. Because people cannot absorb huge chunks of information at a time, give them only as much as they can comfortably digest.
3. The CAT must focus the messages on the target audience. Understand where the audience falls on the cycle of communications. Define the issue. Tell audience members why they should care. Give them a specific action that fits their level of interest. Tell them steps that they can take to advance the cause of your organization.
4. In building messages, the CAT should develop guidelines to help the board, staff, volunteers and other spokespeople:
   1. Try to use the word "you" in at least one of the messages. Persuasive messages need to resonate with people on an individual and personal level, especially if you want to engage them or get them to act.
   2. Ensure that the messages have impact, are irrefutable, are strong, and touch people. The best messages are visceral rather than intellectual. The messages need to speak to people's own personal experiences.
   3. Encourage spokespeople to determine when to speak to the heart and when to speak to the head. If you are making an emotional appeal and you choose to speak in statistics, you face the danger that people will simply stop listening. When you are making a rational appeal, limit the use of human narrative and use it for additional emphasis, not as the central message point.
   4. Language is critical to good messages. Too many people develop potentially great messages but blunt their power by using empty words or jargon. For example, *agency* and *services* are not words that have much of an emotional impact on anyone. Consider the impact of your words on your audience. Do they convey any emotional feeling? If you are talking about the "services" you offer, describe them. Saying "feeding homeless people" and "sharing the love of reading with children" has much more impact than saying "We offer a broad range of services." Give concrete examples.

5. The CAT is responsible for enforcing message discipline. Once the messages have been developed, ensure that everyone knows what they are and uses them consistently. You and your colleagues may get tired of the same message, but do not assume that your audience has absorbed it. According to marketing guru Jay Levinson, a message needs to be received 27 times before it actually registers with the recipient.

Worksheet 14   Simple Framing Analysis

1. State the organization's mission.

2. Identify the four key themes for the organization:

3. How does the organization frame the issue?
   a. What is the problem/cause/solution?
   b. Is this framing:_____ Episodic _____ Thematic
   c. Where is action needed:
   _____ public policy: _____
   _____ community: _____
   _____ individuals: _____

4. How do other organizations frame the issue?
   a. What is the problem/cause/solution?

   b. Is this framing:_____Episodic_____Thematic
   c. Where is action needed:
   _____ public policy: _____
   _____ community: _____
   _____ individuals: _____

5. How does the media frame the issue?
   a. Is there more than one public frame?
   b. What is the problem/cause/solution?

   c. Is this framing:_____ Episodic_____ Thematic
   d. Where is action needed:
   _____ public policy: _____
   _____ community: _____
   _____ individuals: _____

Worksheet 15   Framing Analysis Worksheet

Name of Publication/Source _____

Title _____

Date _____

Is the piece: _____ editorial_____news feature_____ story

1. What spokespeople are mentioned?

2. What is the core position of the article?

3. What catchphrases are used?

4. How does the piece describe the problem/cause/solution?

5. Is the framing:_____ Episodic_____ Thematic

6. How does the piece characterize the source of the problem?

7. How does the piece characterize the solution to the problem?

8. What does the piece predict the outcome will be?

9. What are the core principles underlying the piece?

10. What's not being said? Where are the inconsistencies in the arguments being advanced in the piece?

Worksheet 16   Language Worksheet

Words Currently Used to Describe Our Organization or the Work We Do

Words to Avoid When Talking about Our Organization and the Work that It Does

New Words that Could Have the Greatest Impact on Our Target Audiences

TIPS: Test each word: Does it convey an emotion? Does it have impact? Does it have meaning to civilians? Is it persuasive?

Worksheet 17   Organization Description

Current Organization Description

What impression does the organization want to make?

What themes describe what the organization wants everyone to know about it?

1.
2.
3.
4.

New 20- to 25-Word Organization Description

Worksheet 18   Develop Persuasive Messages

Create a three-part message for each priority audience. It should identify the issue and desired change, make it relevant to the audience, and provide an action step that can be taken. Then write the message as a complete sentence or two. Try to use the most persuasive language and use the word "*you*" at least once.

Target Audience: _____

Desired Change: _____

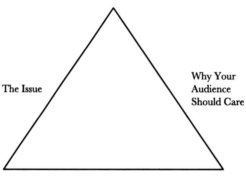

Part 1 (The Issue)

_____

_____

_____

_____

Part 2 (Why Your Audience Should Care)

_____

_____

_____

_____

Part 3 (What You Want Your Audience to Do, Think, or Feel)

_____

_____

_____

_____

Now write a message combining all 3 parts as if you are talking to the audience.

_____

_____

_____

_____

Worksheet 19   Put a Human Face on Your Work

One anecdote about our work that puts a "human face" on our project is:

_____

_____

_____

_____

_____

_____

Another anecdote about our work that puts a "human face" on our project is:

_____

_____

_____

_____

_____

_____

Step Six: Advancing the Plan Vehicles and Dissemination Strategies

Every strategy—and the vehicles used to facilitate each one—has unique attributes that make it attractive to different audiences at different times. What may be a positive strategy at a certain time with a given audience may have a negative effect with that same audience at a different time. A simple example is a phone call. Although people at work expect phone calls from those they do not know (new vendors, potential clients, or volunteers), those same people might not appreciate phone calls from strangers while they are at home (from telemarketing companies, political campaigns asking for money, market researchers).

Criteria for Selecting Strategies

Seven criteria can be used to determine the appropriateness of different strategies with different audiences. In different situations, some criteria will be more important to consider than others. All are factors that influence the eventual success of any communications strategy. The seven criteria are:

1. Audience responsiveness
2. The organization's relationship to the audience
3. How the strategy or vehicle will influence the audience's perception
4. Controlling the message
5. Effort to implement
6. Budget issues
7. Potential uses with other audiences

Audience Responsiveness

Although audience responsiveness may seem an obvious criterion in light of earlier chapters, the day-to-day routines and experiences of their world will determine how receptive audience members will be to a given strategy or vehicle. It is within these parameters—their day-to-day lives—that the nonprofit organization will communicate with them. Some things to consider when deciding the appropriateness of different strategies and vehicles for target audiences are outlined next.

Guiding Questions

- At what time of the day is our audience likely to be most receptive to our approach? (When will our message be welcomed as opposed to being perceived as an intrusion or extraneous?)
- What communications vehicles are they likely to encounter?
- Of those, which ones will they stop and notice?
- Of those, which are they likely to spend time with?
- Of those, which are likely to influence them? Which are they likely to look at more than once? Which are they likely to share with others?

The Organization's Relationship to the Audience

Often a specific strategy will be effective only if the organization has a relationship—or, at the very least, an understanding—with an audience member. Unsolicited communications are likely to be ignored or discarded. For example, an e-mail or fax broadcast sent to someone who has not asked to be on the list or has never before responded to the organization is likely to be disregarded by the recipient, because e-mails and faxes imply an agreed-on relationship. Unsolicited mailings or phone calls, although a common practice, are also unlikely to prompt a significant response rate.

When an organization relies on an "outreach partner" or other third-party messenger (such as the press), it must consider not only its relationship to that third party (who also comprises an audience) but also the relationship of that messenger to the primary target audience. For example, the relationship between the daily newspaper and your target audience (does the audience read this daily newspaper?) will be just as important to consider as the organization's own relationship to reporters and editors at the newspaper. If the organization does not have a relationship with someone at the paper, it will be more difficult to count on that messenger to deliver your message in part or as a whole.

Guiding Questions

- What is the relationship of this audience to our organization?
- Has our organization communicated with this person/audience before?

- If yes, how frequently do we communicate?
- If yes, what has been the nature of our previous communication?
- What can be done to build on the existing relationship?

How the Strategy or Vehicle Will Influence the Audience's Perceptions

Perceptions are at the heart of each individual's opinions, beliefs, and value systems. They are a mix of rational thought and emotional experience. Different communication strategies can influence the audience's perception of the organization and its objective. The communications objective will dictate whether it is better to take a more emotional approach or to use a strategy that speaks to the more rational side of a person's experience. How the issue is framed in the public's perception, how other organizations portray the issue, and how the organization's social and political environment intersects with that of the target audience also must be considered when weighing the potential impact of different strategies.

Consider how you might perceive a housing crisis. A newspaper article provides a wealth of details, perhaps a picture or two, and can give an in-depth understanding of the crisis. Now imagine that same story covered on the six o'clock news—perhaps a 90-second story with clips of homeless people huddled together against the cold and policy makers debating legislation, followed by a clip of the mayor climbing out of his limousine offering his views on the matter. The juxtaposition of these "live" visual images will have a very different effect on the audience's perception of the problem and the appropriate solutions.

Another strategy might be to conduct a town meeting that brings together not only the people most affected by the housing crisis but those who have the ability to do something about it. Audiotaping the meeting and sending out edited versions will create another type of understanding in the target audience—*less* emotional than the video treatment but likely *more* emotional than the print story.

If you use a third party to deliver your message, consider how their role or status in the community may color the target audience's perception. The press validates and lends weight to issues that it covers, with most people perceiving a certain objectivity in the facts presented. If people in the target audience are members of another organization, they may respond more readily to hearing *your* message from *their* organization. The reputation of the messenger influences the reception to and perception of the message.

Guiding Questions

- Will this particular audience be moved by a more rational approach to the issue or by a more emotional telling of the message?
- In the past, has this topic or issue been framed primarily in a rational way, an emotional way, or some combination of the two?
- How would a certain type of documentation (videotape of factory emissions versus audio storytelling versus print fact sheet) tell the same story with different results?
- Does this audience need help visualizing the problem?
- Does this audience need help understanding the facts that are causing this problem?
- Does this audience need help thinking through possible solutions to the problem?
- Does this audience need a more direct experience of the problem (e.g., to interact with staff, volunteers) to feel more connected to it?

Controlling the Message

A message is controlled at both ends of the information exchange: by the producer of the message and by the recipient. The producer can be the organization, someone the organization hires, or third parties with no connection to the organization (e.g., the press). As the producer role moves farther and farther away from the organization's control, so too does the certainty that the message will accurately reflect the organization's perspective.

For example, an organization with an in-house editorial staff may produce reports, Web site pages, and op-eds that literally *are* the voice of the organization. When the organization hires a freelance writer or video producer, staff members can brief her about the issue and give her background materials and people to talk to; but in the end, the freelancer will write or produce in a different voice—perhaps saying what the organization wants to say, but not in the same voice as the in-house staff. When an organization presents material to a reporter during an interview or a press conference, the end result will be a mix of the organization's message and facts with other messages and facts identified independently by the reporter. The reporting may or may not reflect your message accurately. And no matter how accurate or sympathetic the article may be, it will certainly not reflect the voice of the organization.

The other end of message control is even more elusive, because the recipients—readers, viewers, listeners, users, participants—will interpret the message based on their own experiences, prejudices, opinions, attitudes, values, and beliefs. An organization has little direct control over how the audience receives the message. That is why doing research to understand the target audience ensures that the messages and communications vehicles focus like a laser beam at that audience group. Follow-up interviews and monitoring are essential measures to make sure the message is interpreted as the organization meant it to be and that the desired actions were taken.

Guiding Questions

- How important is it to tell the story broadly versus telling it precisely (from the organization's point of view)?
- Which vehicles does the nonprofit currently produce that clearly reflect the voice of the organization?
- Does the organization tend to favor one vehicle over other possible vehicles (e.g., more print than audio, more e-mail than video)?
- If so, why is this better (for the audience; for staff convenience; due to the complexity of the message)?
- What can the organization do to help ensure that the target audience interprets the message accurately (possible feedback mechanisms, interactive follow-up opportunities)?

Effort to Implement

Part of choosing appropriate vehicles for each message is taking into account the complexity of tasks needed to implement the various strategies, the amount of time it will take to complete and disseminate each vehicle and whose time will be taken up in doing it. Further, it is only one of the strategies that needs to be considered; the entire plan needs to be looked at as a whole.

It may be that certain strategies should be postponed. The time spent may seem well worth the effort expended, but there are just too many other things that must get done during the period in which this strategy was originally planned. If so, consider whether the same strategy will be as effective later as it would have been with the original schedule.

Frequently organizations commit to a complex strategy—or even something "simple," such as a monthly newsletter—without assessing how much staff time it will take to accomplish all the tasks involved. The result is unrealistic (and often unmet) deadlines. How can an organization judge if the effort is worth the impact it expects?

Guiding Questions

- How much lead time does the staff have or need before the vehicle will be used?
- How much time will it take staff to produce this vehicle?
- Will each staff member involved work exclusively on this project? If not, how will their other work affect these deadlines?
- Will the production team need to bring in outside help to meet the deadline?
- If a consultant will be used or the press will be approached to package the message, how much time will it take for the staff to initiate, follow up, and work with these outside individuals to ensure that the message is delivered as closely as possible to what the organization desires?

Budget Issues

A strategy is appropriate only if it is affordable. If it looks as if costs can be covered and the time demands met, consider out-of-pocket expenses, such as graphic design, postage, telephone charges, room rentals, travel, speakers' fees, and refreshments. At this stage, it is less important to tally a detailed budget than it is to estimate the range of costs for each project and, given that range, determine if the strategies are truly a good option for the organization.

Although there is no magic formula for a communications budget, most of the more successful nonprofits, large and small, work with a communications budget that is 8% to 12% of their total organizational budget. Many advocacy groups exceed the high end of that range. Unfortunately, most organizations do not consider their total spending on communications functions and, as a result, do not allow themselves room to reallocate costs from one type of strategy to another, more effective strategy. For example, instead of doing a first-class mailing of a one-page memo or letter to 300 people, consider an ezine, blog, or e-mail at considerably less cost.

Guiding Questions

- Is this the most important communications priority within our budget? If not, where does it fall?
- Is the cost of this strategy realistic for the size of the organization's budget?
- Is there a way to reallocate existing resources to realize a bigger bang for the buck?
- Can additional money be raised if needed for this strategy or vehicle? (How much time would it take to secure that type of contribution? Does the organization have the time to raise it? Is that time well spent?)

- Are there ways that costs associated with this strategy could be defrayed through in-kind contributions? (How much time would it take to secure that type of contribution? Does the organization have the time? Is that time well spent?)

Potential Uses with Other Audiences

Organizations that tailor messages to their specific audience are most likely to have success in reaching their targeted communications objective. However, with careful strategic thinking, it can be possible to save staff time and money by adapting a given strategy to serve multiple audiences. Clustering audiences that have similar information needs or from whom you desire the same type of action (write your legislator) can allow the organization to craft messages and/or develop brochures and other materials that are appropriate for multiple purposes.

For example, many national magazines put different covers on the same issue in order to attract different audiences, without changing the information inside. If a single report is of interest to diverse audiences, consider using different cover sheets or including targeted executive summaries. Doing this eliminates the need to rewrite the report to fit each audience's interests yet still appeals to individual concerns.

Guiding Questions

- Is this an event or strategy that would appeal to different audience groups? If yes, can the staff ensure that they are exposed to the messages most appropriate to their concerns?
- Do several audience groups read the same publication, listen to the same radio program, watch the same television program?
- Can the writers easily tailor the headline and first paragraph to better address another audience group?
- If there is "something for everyone" in the message, is it presented in a way that allows members of different audience groups to find what they are looking for easily?

Evaluating Existing and Potential Strategies for Meeting Communications Objectives

Worksheet 20 outlines the process for evaluating potential communications strategies. The communications action team (CAT) will want to review the strategic options under consideration and assign a numeric value (from 1 to

5, with 5 being the highest) for the effectiveness of each strategy against the seven criteria in this way:

1. *Responsive to Audience:* 1 unresponsive, 5 highly responsive
2. *Appropriate Relationship:* 1 inappropriate, 5 builds on our strengths
3. *Strategy Affects Perception:* 1 emotional, 5 rational
4. *Strategy Affects Message:* 1 no control over message, 5 we control message
5. *Effort to Implement:* 1 draws on our strengths, 5 will tax our capacity
6. *Cost to Implement:* 1 least expensive, 5 most expensive
7. *Impact on Others:* 1 no impact on others, 5 allows us to reach other targeted audiences

The numeric score gives the CAT a basis for comparing the various options under consideration, but the final score does not indicate which strategy is necessarily the right strategy for the organization. Decide which strategies are the most likely to give you the desired result with the target audience while also considering the amount of staff time and financial resources that will be required. Do not make final decisions at this time. Rank order (from 1 to 5) the effective strategies for this target audience and this strategic communications objective. After the CAT completes this process for all of the goals and objectives in the strategic plan, it will be able to make final decisions regarding which strategies and vehicles to include.

Case Study: Future Generations

Future Generations is committed to helping the next generation be born free from chronic healthcare problems and learning disabilities. An important objective is to inform parents about the effects of alcohol on adolescent development. The nonprofit has been trying to build awareness of the issue among a specific group of parents, laying the foundation for a more proactive commitment to alcohol abuse prevention efforts on a personal as well as a community level. Five possible strategies are under consideration:

1. Conduct a series of evening forums with experts to provide research findings and factual information and parent activists who can share their experiences. The forums can be videotaped and provided to local media as well as to parents who are unable to attend the forums.

2. Send monthly mailings that will alert parents to the problem of adolescent alcohol use and abuse and include a "talk to your kids" guide sheet.

3. Set up information tables at the local grocery store and malls, recruiting students to hand out leaflets and bumper stickers.

4. Have several students perform skits that present the issue in a dramatic way at the fall PTA meeting.

5. Conduct training sessions about adolescents and alcohol abuse for junior high teachers so that they can talk about the subject with parents during parent-teacher conferences.

By considering how effective each strategy will be with the specific audience group, Future Generations staff will be able to evaluate and prioritize these strategies using the seven criteria outlined earlier.

1. *Audience responsiveness.* Most parents in the school district do not work in the evening, so they could be available to attend evening forums or parent-teacher conferences. Monthly information packets via first-class mail are guaranteed to reach the parents in the home and can be read at each person's convenience. Similarly, leafleting at the mall or grocery store also guarantees that the information will reach the parents, although it is less clear whether the material will actually be read. A follow-up phone call or classroom assignment that requires the child to engage the parent in a discussion might be needed to make these strategies effective.

2. *Organization's relationship to the audience.* Future Generations is a 25-year-old organization that has worked in the region to create healthy and safe communities. It is well known and well respected. Based on the organization's positive and proactive connection to the community, the evening forums, the monthly mailings, and the leaflets are most likely to be seen as valid, informed, and connected to Future Generations. The other two strategies—parent-teacher conferences and PTA meetings—rely more on the relationship between the parent and the teacher and the school as well as the relationship among Future Generations, the school district, and individual schools. Thus, these strategies are appropriate as well, with the school reinforcing the value of the work of Future Generations.

3. *Strategy influences perceptions.* The evening forums and the PTA meetings provide forums where parents can socialize and interact with other parents around an issue of mutual concern. Being approached by students in the grocery store or shopping center may also catch the

attention of parents and suggest some urgency. These approaches are likely to have some emotional resonance as well as provide practical information. The monthly mailings may or may not attract the attention necessary to encourage parental action.

4. *Strategy affects the message.* In all of these strategies, Future Generations controls the message with the target audience. In the monthly mailings and the leaflets, Future Generations develops the information that is provided. In the other forums, Future Generations has created the format and provided talking points. The question here is really one about who will be the most effective messenger with the parents who have been targeted.

5. *Effort to implement.* The amount of staff time and talent varies across each of these five strategies. The evening forum, with the logistics and material preparation, is the most staff-intensive strategy. The parent-teacher meetings would take the least amount of effort, since the organization has to brief the teachers only once, which it could do through available print and video materials. The student skits at the PTA meetings would take fewer resources than the leafleting project, since the skits could be managed on an as-needed basis. The monthly mailings would have to be written, produced, collated, and mailed every month—requiring a manageable investment of energy by the staff.

6. *Budget issues.* In addition to staff time, financial concern is often the deciding factor for many nonprofits when making strategic choices. The least expensive strategy in this example would be the PTA meeting and the parent-teacher conferences. Expenses for the leafleting strategy would be just above that; the evening forums (with outside experts, speakers' travel costs, promotional expenses, and rented space) are the most expensive.

7. *Potential impact on other groups.* There is little likelihood that the leaflets would be circulated to other audiences. Similarly, parent-teacher conferences are private discussions that are not likely be discussed with others. The skits at PTA meetings might involve a larger circle of community members, teachers, and parents in a discussion of potential community responses. Reporters may cover the event and print a piece in the local paper.

As Exhibit 8.1 shows, the staff can assign a rating on a scale of 1 to 5 to each of these seven variables to determine relative value for the strategies under consideration. As the ratings on Exhibit 8.1 show, the PTA meetings rank as the biggest bang for the buck, while the forums are regarded as requiring a lot of staff effort and expense without a perceptibly larger impact on the target audiences. The leafleting and monthly mailings are regarded

Exhibit 8.1 Future Generations Evaluation of Strategic Options

Step 1. Review the strategic options under consideration and assign a numeric value (from 1 to 5, with 5 being the highest) for the effectiveness of each strategy against the seven criteria.

  1. *Responsive to audience:* 1 unresponsive, 5 highly responsive
  2. *Appropriate relationship:* 1 inappropriate, 5 builds on our strengths
  3. *Strategy affects perception:* 1 emotional, 5 rational
  4. *Strategy affects message:* 1 no control over message, 5 we control message
  5. *Effort to implement:* 1 draws on our strengths, 5 will tax our capacity
  6. *Cost to implement:* 1 least expensive, 5 most expensive
  7. *Impact on others:* 1 no impact on others, 5 allows us to reach other targeted audiences

Step 2. Decide which strategies are the most likely to give you the desired result with the target audience.
Step 3. Rank order the effective strategies for this target audience and this strategic communications objective.

Targeted Audience: High School Parents

Strategy	Responsive to audience	Appropriate relationship	Strategy affects perception	Strategy affects message	Effort to implement	Cost to implement	Impact on other audiences	Total	Rank order
Evening forum with guest speakers and parents as panellists	2	1	3	2	5	5	5	23	3
Monthly mailings	1	2	3	1	3	4	1	15	4
Parent-teacher meetings	2	2	1	4	1	2	5	17	2
Leafleting at grocery store and the shopping mall by students	4	3	4	3	4	3	2	23	5
Student skits at the PTA meeting	2	2	2	4	2	1	3	16	1

The evening forums turn out to be a lot of effort and expensive, which may not offset the other positive values. The parent-teacher meetings are low on message control and impact on others, even though the strategy is very cost effective. Leafleting is not exceptionally effective on any measure. Monthly mailings score low on message control, cost, and impact. The PTA meetings provide the biggest bank for the buck—they are most effective in advancing the communications objective and using the organization's human and other resources wisely.

as low impact, even though the information provided could be used to support the forum, the parent-teacher conferences, and the PTA briefings.

Case Study: Planet 3000

Planet 3000 is planning to mobilize small business owners from 75 congressional districts in 6 pilot cities to support a comprehensive transportation/ clean air policy initiative. Some strategies developed by the staff for consideration include:

1. Conducting a poll to assess depth of support for this policy among the targeted audience group and alternative community actions for ensuring passage of the legislation. The findings would be released at a press conference held in conjunction with the National Chambers of Commerce Annual Meeting. Potential for making the legislation a national policy priority for the Chambers and expand the pilot project for Year 2.
2. Distribute radio actualities and video news releases (VNRs) highlighting the poll findings to focus attention on the impact of traffic on air quality and the air quality standards in the proposed legislation and to solicit community participation through local Chambers.
3. Host town hall meetings in advance of the annual meeting, circulating petitions and gathering support for the legislation. Business accounts of how they are changing the way that they do business will provide more incentives for legislators to support "proven practices."
4. Recruit a "celebrity" spokesperson to present at the National Chambers of Commerce Annual Meeting in Washington, DC. Do a satellite media tour and a "Lobby Day" on Capitol Hill, with media escorting the celebrity spokesperson to select Member offices.
5. Create a home page for the business-for-business campaign with links to local groups in the 75 targeted congressional districts. Encourage peer-to-peer sharing of strategies and successes in engaging community business partners and meeting with local officials. Templates for the town meetings and other tools could also be posted for the pilot projects.

Here are the staff's findings on each of the seven criteria:

1. *Audience Responsiveness*
   The poll will not only help staff assess the target audience's opinions more accurately but provides additional grassroots credibility for work with the Chamber and policy makers. Local reporters and media

outlets in the targeted districts will also have the data to supplement the human face that we will put on the story through the town hall meetings.

Planet 3000 staff also expects the target audience will be responsive because of the link to the national Chambers' interest and the endorsement of their local chapters. The celebrity spokesperson will also add credibility with the target audience and cache for this initiative.

The Web strategy also provides friendly peer-to-peer competition across the pilot projects and can demonstrate local successes, making it harder for those involved to say "This can't be done." The combination of all this local effort and activity will help demonstrate to policy makers and others the growing strength of the movement and the support behind the passing of the proposed legislation.

2. *Organization's Relationship to the Audience*
Planet 3000 does not have any current relationship with the local small business communities that have been targeted. It is relying on its relationship with the national Chambers and its outreach partnerships to make this initiative happen. While these relationships appear strong, there is a lot riding on the targeting of the right pilot cities and the right community partners. There will be pressure on the Planet 3000 staff to make sure that the project is well managed and pleasurable for all the partners involved.

Planet 3000 will continue to work with the National Chamber of Commerce and cultivate members of the business press. By conducting the poll and the local impact information, Planet 3000 serves the business community while advancing its mission and policy agenda.

3. *Strategy Influences Perception*
The National Chamber of Commerce endorsement of this effort and the use of business-focused arguments and rationales create a natural synergy that should excite local businesses. The challenge for Planet 3000 will be to ensure continued momentum and the sense that this partnership is local and beneficial to both. We will want to minimize too much emphasis on the research part of our organization and highlight the advocacy and activism of the grassroots business partners.

The approach is based on a strongly rational model, framed in economic and business terms about the bottom line. Planet 3000 will highlight the links between the policy guidelines and its support of local business interests. By relying on the business press, the Chambers of Commerce, and local reporters to deliver the message,

Planet 3000 hopes to reach other businesses, their vendor partners, and their customers, greatly expanding the base of support for the legislation and the outreach to policy makers.

4. *Strategy Affects the Message*
Planet 3000 will have some control over the message through the survey data and the Web site, but the organization has made a calculated decision to rely on local business leaders, the Chambers, and other business interests to be the major spokespeople in this initiative. The organization will have to ensure that all spokespeople stay on message, reinforcing key points as well as the desired frame that will effectively position the issue and the stories in the media. Even the radio actuality and the VNR will be important pieces of the strategy for "staying on message."

The fact that the target audience will be more receptive to messages delivered by these spokespeople outweighs the limited control that Planet 3000 will have over how the message unfolds during the campaign. The engagement materials and the Web site, while reaching the primary audience in its original form, will also be used and modified by the local groups in ways that will go beyond the organization's control.

5. *Effort to Implement*
Planet 3000 has spent the past 6 months building the bridges that are necessary to make these strategies happen. It also has a 5-person communications and public affairs team that will manage and implement the strategies. A working team with 3 representatives from each of the pilot sites has also been meeting regularly by conference call for the past 3 months and will start meeting weekly once the campaign is launched. There will be an outside consultant working full time to manage the growth of the Web site and to monitor the Web interaction during the campaign.

6. *Budget Issues*
The strategies proposed are both high profile and expensive, but the organization sees this initiative as crucial to building its credibility and its base of support at the business, community, and national policy level. The board and senior leadership are committed to the campaign and have worked with funders and individual donors to build support for this initiative. The staff expects to keep the costs of the VNR to a minimum by using existing footage from its library and from local sources. It has negotiated a discounted package with the satellite feed company that will transmit the actuality and the VNR. Relying on Web transmissions of materials means that the local businesses and

local Chambers will absorb many of the production costs for materials. The poll is also an expensive item, but it is serving a dual function regarded as essential to the campaign: shaping the actual messages and strategies and generating credibility with the press, the National Chamber of Commerce, and elected officials.

7. *Potential Impact on Other Audiences*
All of these strategies are designed to reach multiple audiences. It is hoped that they will reach the business press, business partners and vendors, and customers. Targeted petitions, letters, and messages to Congress will be generated and will hopefully advance the policy agenda through passage of comprehensive legislation.

Worksheet 20, found at the end of this chapter, can be used to evaluate strategic options.

Strategies and Vehicles to Meet Communications Objectives

Communications objectives, taken singly or together, are likely to involve several strategies and vehicles before they are completed. Each communications vehicle, targeted to a specific audience, is a step toward the actual completion of the objective. Ideally, strategies and vehicles build on each other, with the cumulative effect helping to realize both program goals and the organizational mission. This section takes a close look at available communications vehicles and factors to consider in evaluating how well they might meet the needs outlined by the organization in its strategic communications plan.

Face-to-Face Meetings

Face-to-face meetings or events convey immediacy about an issue or message, because things happen in "real time" and in a "shared space." Because participants are able to read each other's body language and look into each other's eyes, they are more likely to recognize misunderstandings, listen to opposing viewpoints, and challenge their own suppositions based on the perceived sincerity of the other participants. Because of this, face-to-face is one of the best ways to engage individuals to work through complex or conflicting attitudes, opinions, and beliefs about an issue, problem, or concern.

Face-to-face strategies can influence two different audience groups simultaneously: the participants and the observers. For example, an organization convenes a summit where experts present papers and discuss the latest trends. While the experts are involved in developing a consensus, the press, policy makers, community leaders, or other decision makers are becoming more aware of the problem.

Because it is expensive to bring people together, in terms of both time and money, face-to-face strategies convey the impression that "something is happening here." When participants at a face-to-face meeting or event generate enough energy and enthusiasm for action, it is easier to get others to take action as well.

Types of Face-to-Face Vehicles

Lunch	Legislative site visits	Media tours
Press conferences	Focus groups	Workshops
Interviews	Press briefings	Conferences, seminars
Board meetings	Editorial board meetings	Speeches

Benefits of Face-to-Face Meetings

- They establish personal relationships through direct contact.
- They allow the convenors to read the situation through eye/body contact.
- They are best for intensive experiences such as training, consensus building, and conflict resolution.
- They can, and should, incorporate other vehicles (e.g., print, video, PowerPoint, audio).

Challenges of Face-to-Face Meetings

- Logistics are important (adequate space, good lighting, ease of access).
- Ground rules for interaction must be established (will the meeting be off the record, who will be allowed to speak, will there be time for questions and answers?).
- The meetings require both formal (structured) and informal networking (unstructured) time.
- In planning events, the CAT should consider an invitation-only event versus open events. (Are there some groups, such as the press or opposition groups, that should not be involved at this time?)

Guiding Questions

- Who is/are the target audience(s) for this event? Are there other priority audiences that ought to be included as well?
- How will this vehicle communicate the organization's message?
- Will this activity alienate any of the strategic targets reflected in the overall plan or hurt the organization's overall credibility?
- Does the nonprofit's budget reflect the time, money, and people necessary to implement this strategy, and is it worth the investment?
- If the plan highlights the need for press attention, is this event really newsworthy?
- How can coalition partners contribute to this effort (in terms of money, people, and connections)?
- Will it engage and inspire target audiences?
- Is it simple, achievable, and effective?
- Will this event set up the organization for the next round of activities, in terms of strengthening the organization, creating demand and/or accountability, and building momentum?

Rules of the Road: Face-to-Face Meetings

1. If possible, the event planners should allow time for the people involved to network with each other, share experiences, and reestablish or cement existing ties.
2. The event planners should always ask participants to make a specific commitment at the time of the event.
3. The event planners should give participants materials before they leave the meeting to reinforce their experiences, and make sure they have contact information for other participants, presenters, and representatives of the sponsoring organization.
4. The event planners should remember that the human dynamic—combining diverse knowledge bases, priorities, personalities, opinions, beliefs, and attitudes—can trigger unexpected positive as well as negative outcomes. Be prepared by anticipating the responses of different people who will be in attendance.
5. The event planners should consider various formats, remembering that:
   - A large advantage of invitation-only events is that the organization can control the guest lists.
   - People self-select to attend meetings or events that are open to the public, often making it impossible for the host organization to control what messages attendees remember.

- The format is important. Selecting a format should be guided by ground rules. In this way, the organization can control the agenda if conflicting attitudes disrupt the meeting. Have a detailed agenda so participants understand the ground rules.
- Be aware that the press often interprets events through the lens of "conflict." A public meeting hosted to air differing opinions and discuss divergent views may be covered in terms of the conflict rather than the substance of the issue itself.

Print

Nonprofits tend to rely more heavily on print than on other types of media to create and sustain relationships with their audiences. Print is familiar and accessible to most audiences in our society. Producers of print materials and most readers/viewers are comfortable with the medium.

Print vehicles rely on visual impact and delivery method to get the audience's attention. Once the connection is made, content and other elements sustain the reader's attention. Over time, print materials can establish a relationship between the producer and the reader; examples of such successful print pieces include the *New York Times, Newsweek,* and some professional journals and organizational newsletters.

To use print effectively, it is helpful to note some realities about how most audiences respond to the medium:

- Brochures have about 3 seconds to capture the reader's attention.
- Direct mail pieces have about 11 seconds to engage the reader.
- Captions with pictures are read 70% more often than regular text.
- Most readers will look at the front and then the back before turning their attention to the rest of a printed piece.

For the most part, print is a one-way medium—a solitary experience intended for individual audience members. Seven elements are used to attract readers to print:

1. *Photos.* A picture is worth a thousand words, and it puts the human face in the message. The right photo can draw an audience's attention, even before the headlines.
2. *Photo captions and pull quotes.* Captions with pictures are read 70% more frequently than all other copy. Pull quotes—highlighted ideas without pictures—often are used to reinforce key points or ideas that give a sort of executive summary of key points in an article.

3. *Headlines/titles.* Boldness and brevity capture a reader's attention in a few seconds while conveying the essence of the story in a nutshell. If the headlines do not sing to the reader, it is unlikely that they will read the rest of the article.

4. *Design.* If a print piece looks interesting, it is likely to attract a reader's attention. If a piece is designed so that it is easy to read, it is more likely to be read. If a piece is unusual in its size, shape, or weight, it is more likely to be noticed.

5. *Sidebars/boxes.* Separating key points in a document and setting them off from the main text guides a reader's eye to that segment of text. These blocked pieces of text can also be used to attach related material to make a long piece appear shorter.

6. *Graphs and charts.* These visual representations help underscore key messages in longer pieces. Graphs and charts help readers more readily understand data and its significance.

7. *Color.* People unconsciously respond to color, and the meanings of color are constantly reinforced by our culture—for example, red is associated with anger, heat, energy; blue is interpreted as cool, calm, stable; green represents envy as well as environmental concerns. Color can be used to call attention to a message or to reinforce a theme.

Print does not allow real-time interaction with audience members. Print is a durable medium. The target audience can retain and consult a printed piece at a time and in a manner that works best for them. The organization has relatively little control over when and how the audience interacts with the printed matter and often does not know the audience's reaction to the printed piece.

Types of Print Vehicles

Novelty items	Press releases	Brochures
Posters	Advertising	Reports/white papers
Feature stories	Direct mail	Annual reports
Fact sheets	Surveys	Op-ed pieces
Proposals	Letters to the editors	Editorials
Magazine, journal, newsletter articles		

Benefits of Print Material

- It is familiar and accessible for most people.
- It is easy to use with audiences and portable.

- It is easy to provide details, terminology, and graphics in print material.
- Print material has a lengthy shelf life and is ready for future reference.
- It is essential for conveying complete and detailed information.

Challenges of Print Material

- Printed matter is of limited use with people who cannot read or have difficulty reading, or when there is a language barrier.
- It offers no audio or personal interaction.
- The audience cannot respond directly.
- Costs of print materials can be high.

Guiding Questions

- Is this target audience comfortable with print materials?
- Is the strategy to have the audience take away the materials and refer to them later? Is there a response card with the materials?
- How do we make the print materials visually exciting and interesting?
- Do we have the resources to develop well-written, engaging, and visually attractive materials?
- Can the materials be used with different audiences?
- How long a shelf life will these print materials have?
- Have we considered how to use our print materials to brand the organizational identity and mission in the audience's minds?

Rules of the Road: Print Vehicles

1. In designing print vehicles, the communications staff must remember these guidelines.
   - Less is always more. Catch readers' attention and whet their appetite for more.
   - Successful communication vehicles make a connection with the audience, affect an audience emotionally, and brand the organization's identity in the audience's perception.
   - Strong, clear design (just like sloppy, dull design) produces a visceral reaction in the audience.
   - For the most impact, develop a graphic identity that visually expresses the organization's mission. A graphic theme creates an "organizational look"

that has continuity and becomes recognizable by key audiences. A graphic identity uses consistent logo design, typeface, color, and paper.

- Be sure that the graphics (especially the logo) are simple, attractive, and emotionally appealing. Graphics should be symbolic of the organization and print and reproduce well.
- Use words sparingly and effectively, relying on language that has emotional appeal and is clear and precise. Make every word count.
- Develop print materials that are "evergreen" and versatile--those that have a long shelf life and can be used over time —but do not try to make one piece all things to all people. Consider whether the print material will stand alone or be used to support other communication vehicles.
- Print has a unique capacity for handling and presenting details, complex facts, and statistical data—but do not attempt to make every point or cover every issue in detail. Do not overwhelm readers.

2. Always keep in mind that print materials themselves are not the goal of strategic communications. Print is a vehicle for achieving organizational goals.

Electronic Communications

In some ways, e-mail is still a puzzling phenomenon. Nearly all professionals are firmly hooked into e-mail as part of their jobs, but there are wide variations in how the vehicle is used. Doctors and lawyers, for example, seem to share their e-mail addresses with patients/clients only rarely. Educators and, more recently, politicians are at the opposite extreme and encourage e-mail from students and constituents. Some older people have taken to e-mail as a vehicle ideally suited to their circumstances; others resist learning how to use "the computer." The much-discussed *digital divide* is growing smaller as costs go down, public institutions offer free Internet access, and service providers penetrate rural areas. At the same time, connection speeds (and therefore transmission rates) vary widely, and such traditional barriers as native language and literacy still apply. This patchwork of considerations comes into play when planning how e-mail can convey the organization's messages successfully to key audiences.

By tradition, e-mail is an informal vehicle well suited to exchanging short, friendly messages with people who already have a relationship with the staff or the organization. An advantage e-mail has over other vehicles is that it typically delivers the message directly to the desktop of the audience, without the layers that usually filter phone and mail contacts. (As the amount of junk e-mail grows, however, it is likely e-mail will evolve filtering layers as well.)

E-mail is also a low-cost and efficient method of delivering the message. When used with a relational database that can sort by categories, e-mail allows an organization to target a defined group of people and, with a few keystrokes, send the message to all of them at once. This function is quite useful for broadcasting news announcements, for example, or for tailoring messages to donors at various levels of giving. It is also possible to piggyback document and image files as attachments to e-mails. (It is best to attach files configured in such universal formats as .pdf and .jpg.)

There are various kinds of e-mail forums created to serve people who self-select into audiences around a shared topic or concern. The CAT should research newsgroups, bulletin boards, My Space and other online face pages, blogs, and listservs useful to the organization; the organization can join these forums and post its messages to them. If the right kind of e-mail forum does not exist in your topic area, the organization might consider developing and hosting one. A dedicated staff person is essential to keep e-mail traffic moving and responsive to audience inquiries.

Remember that soliciting and responding to e-mails can be another means of meeting the organization's communications objectives. Print vehicles can include e-mail addresses as a method of responding or requesting more information. E-mail addresses can be posted on the Web site as a hypertext link for easy response. E-mail is also a quick and effective means of soliciting feedback with surveys and other forms of measurement and evaluation.

A drawback worth mentioning is that some people perceive e-mail to be cold and impersonal. This perception can result from an audience's unfamiliarity with the technology (know your audience!) and from the sender's writing style and technique (it is tricky, for example, to convey irony and humor with e-mail). Although few people would consider sending a business letter without a salutation and closing, a surprising number of people skip these courtesies when sending e-mails. A simple greeting (Hi, Amanda—) and closing with your name can soften the impersonal edges of e-mail and keep you from sounding curt or brusque.

Types of E-mail Vehicles

Person to person	Grouped by defined audience	Listserv (host)
Newsgroup	Bulletin or message board	Listserv (post)
Instant messaging		

Rules of the Road: E-mail

1. In designing its electronic communications strategies, the staff should remember these tools:
- Be sure to choose the subject heading strategically. A good subject heading increases the chances that the e-mail will be read. The subject heading also functions as the e-mail's file name, and a descriptive heading will make it easier for your audience to file and later locate a given e-mail.
- By tradition, e-mail is quite friendly and informal. Use this tone and style to the nonprofit's advantage in cultivating audiences.
- If possible, choose an e-mail address that reflects well on the organization. Remember that domain names (e.g., .gov, .edu, .org) carry meaning for your audiences. It is difficult, for example, to raise money using a .gov e-mail address.
- Take full advantage of the ''signature'' function e-mail offers. This is an excellent opportunity to feature the organization's one-line description or tagline. Also consider including a hypertext link to the organization's Web site.
- Never, never, never send or forward large files as attachments unless the audience has asked that you do so.

2. Most importantly, in all of its communications, the staff should remember that courtesy still counts: Always include a salutation and closing.

Benefits of E-mail

- It offers fast desk-to-desk delivery.
- It is useful for sending documents and image transfer (.pdf, .jpg formats).
- It is inexpensive to send and receive.
- It can be audience-targeted.
- E-mail is a highly manageable and accessible technology.

Challenges of E-mail

- Audiences have varying levels of access to the Internet.
- It is sometimes perceived as impersonal.
- It shares some limitations with print (possible language, reading barriers).
- It can be difficult to ''brand'' the organization through the inclusion of the logo, mission statement, organization description, or other

signature pieces of the message platform in the e-mail address. Some organizations encourage all employees to add the organization's tag line to their signature as a way to address this problem.

Guiding Questions

- Are the key audiences likely to respond to this vehicle?
- Are staff members comfortable with this technology and able to use it with fluid ease? Does the organization have clear protocols for using electronic messaging?
- Do we have the equipment and the service connection needed to make e-mail a viable tool for our organization?
- For cost efficiency, what messages should we shift to e-mail delivery (from, e.g., print, audio, face-to-face)? How is the shift likely to affect how our messages are received?

Audio Vehicles

Audio vehicles are inexpensive, generally easy to use, portable, and familiar to almost everyone. Sound is good at conveying emotion, drama, or a sense of urgency; and although it engages only the one sense (hearing), audio can be used effectively to create mental images. It works best with simple messages.

Audio is quite flexible. It can reach a mass audience, a niche audience, or a single person, and do so almost instantaneously. It can help to create a sense of closeness or community—people on a conference call or tuned in to a radio talk show develop a connection much like people meeting face-to-face.

Other desirable aspects of audio include a high degree of message control and compatibility with other communications vehicles. And it is an excellent choice to reach audiences who cannot read print.

Types of Audio Vehicles

Audiotapes	Direct phone calls	Radio talk shows
Message machines	Hotlines, toll-free numbers	Radio ads
Pagers	Teleconferences	Radio community calendars
Music, jingles	Internet streaming	Radio PSAs
Automated prompts	Compact discs	Radio news

Benefits of Audio Vehicles

- They are good at conveying emotion, drama, and urgency.
- They are effective with people who cannot read.
- They can be interactive.
- They can create a sense of personal contact.
- They can reach a large audience quickly.
- They are compatible with other vehicles.

Challenges of Audio Vehicles

- They can be effective for a limited amount of time if they are promoting a specific event or opportunity. In addition, some stations refuse to allow long run times for nonprofit messages.
- It is difficult to convey complex information.
- Some delivery methods can be expensive.
- You need to match the delivery method with the audience's equipment.
- Some audio vehicles might require staff training.

Rules of the Road: Audio Vehicles

The communications staff should consider these general guidelines:
- Because audio vehicles generally work best when the message is straightforward, messages should be clear and concise. If there is a need to convey a lot of complicated information, especially numbers or statistical data, use another vehicle.
- Audio vehicles work best when "narrowcasting," that is, when there is a need to reach a specific, narrow audience. Radio stations, for example, generally have niche audiences based on demographics (e.g., age, income, gender, drive time). Before beginning a radio campaign, for example, an organization must research the audience characteristics of the station(s) that it is considering.
- Use all the qualities of the voice to convey the message; be aware of timbre, pitch, tone, and volume.
- Keep context in mind. Audiences often respond better to information provided as advice or counseling.
- Articulate clearly and use short sentences with active verbs. Repetition is also important, but avoid sounding like a parrot.
- Make sure only one person speaks at a time, to avoid interruptions and "muddying."

Guiding Questions

- Is audio the most effective way to reach this target audience?
- Where is the nonprofit in the communications process with this audience (inform/engage/motivate to act/maintain relationship)? Is an audio vehicle (e.g., a phone call) the best way to go at this stage?
- How will the audio vehicle prompt the audience to act in the desired way?
- Do our communications objectives play to the strengths of an audio vehicle? Is the message simple? Do we need interactivity?
- How will this audio vehicle support/reinforce/complement our other communications efforts?
- Can we do this right? Is it going to involve skills and/or resources we have or can get?

Video

Video is considered a high-impact communications vehicle, because it engages the senses of both seeing and hearing. Indeed, fully half of video's impact comes from sound, whether it is the voices speaking, music, or special sound effects. To avoid a video that is static or includes only "talking heads," work with a producer who can create highly emotional effects and manipulate moving images and sound into the video. Video is an excellent "documentation" tool and is probably the best medium to use when trying to capture the overall experience of a program or project.

In our society, audiences are very comfortable with video, and it can be especially useful with audiences who cannot read. As with all communications vehicles, there may be a need for different versions, such as unique openings or tailored requests at closure, to be successful with different audiences.

Producing a high-quality video vehicle requires very specialized training, and it is essential to rely on people who know how to write, shoot, and edit. And video is often less flexible than other vehicles—partly because the expense of doing it well argues against continually revising or updating it.

When something is presented in video format, it invites the audience to be a participant in what happened. For this reason, it is important to portray events that have actually occurred or that reflect real human experience. This phenomenon requires an ethical approach to how you present information, so that you retain a reputation for being honest and trustworthy. With video, it is especially important to respect the wishes of clients and volunteers who request anonymity or for minors and those with disabilities.

The technology for duplicating video and playing it back has become highly affordable and widely available. Like any other vehicle produced by nonprofits for distribution, it is usually necessary to use *another* vehicle (press release, face-to-face meeting, phone call) to prompt the audience actually to watch the video. Effective video can become the highlight of a meeting or fundraiser or house party, generating useful discussion and even money.

Types of Video Vehicles

Films, trailers	Stand-alone videotape	Network TV
TV news	Video conferencing	Cable TV
Internet streaming	TV ads, PSAs	Community access channels
Cell phone messaging	Closed circuit (hotels)	Live billboards, scoreboards

Benefits of Video

- Most audiences are comfortable with video.
- It can be dramatic, with a visceral effect on an audience.
- It can demonstrate how a program works and show how the organization's work affects real people.
- Most people are moved by visuals.
- A lot of information can be conveyed in a short amount of time.
- It can be portable.
- When combined with satellite distribution in real time, it can create a "global village."
- Video brings the world—for better or worse—into our homes.

Challenges of Video

- It can be expensive to produce.
- People expect high production values.
- It requires great expertise and time to do well.
- Video does not age well.
- Video can have a blurring or numbing effect; keep it short and simple.

Guiding Questions

- Does our organization have something to document or demonstrate that cannot easily be conveyed in some other medium?
- Does the communications budget have enough money to produce a high-quality video? Are resources being pulled from other projects that may be more valuable to our overall plan and objectives?

- Does our organization have access to the expertise (writer, director, camera operator, producer, editor) needed to make this video as good as it can be?
- Can the organization make a video that will resonate with the most important audience(s)? Will the audience actually take the time to watch it?
- Does the organization have a good story to tell?
- How will the organization maximize the distribution and use of this video?
- Will this video help in establishing a brand for the organization and its programs?

Rules of the Road: Video

1. The communications staff should consider these guidelines when developing a videoproduct:
- Success requires an experienced production team that can translate the organization's vision into a short, concise, effective video. The typical team consists of a producer, director, writer, camera operator, sound person, editor, or any combination of these.
- The topic or program should be visual in nature. There is nothing worse than video footage of a "talking head" or segments that lack action and movement.
- Making a video is never cheap, and using university students or donated labor can often be a huge mistake when the goal is a top-quality video. You get what you pay for.
- Be realistic about what the organization wants to accomplish and clear about the reason for producing the video. Good message development and careful selection of images that convey the message are key to success.
- Be aware of the target audience(s). Younger viewers will appreciate a fast pace and lively music, while older viewers may feel overwhelmed by the same techniques.

2. The CAT should consider different ways the video can be used, ways that can leverage the initial investment by editing a single video in different ways to reach different audiences.

Web Sites

Online communications are proactive, interactive, and ongoing. They involve finding and posting relevant information; identifying with current, potential, and seeker (people who are roaming the Web and find the site because the issue interests them) audiences; and, it is hoped, developing an online community. A well-organized, well-written, well-maintained, and graphically compelling Web presence is one of the best ways to educate and influence key constituencies. Web sites tend to develop in three phases: information provision (placeholder sites), information provision with limited membership feedback (sign-up, order materials, etc.), and a fully integrated, interactive site that allows the visitor to interact with the host site. Effective Web sites approach information management in a manner that is light, layered, and linked. That is:

- *Light:* The site is inviting and warm and encourages people to explore. There is enough information on the home page to show that viewers have come to the right location, but not so much that they feel bogged down by the information.
- *Layered:* The site has an index that invites users to delve deeper. It provides easy links back to the home page and cross-references the material within the site.
- *Linked:* Increasingly it is important for viewers to connect with other Web sites that provide related information, auxiliary services, and additional information or to review additional perspectives.

When people refer to *the Internet* (or *the Net*), they usually mean the vast collection of sites available online through the World Wide Web (or *the Web*). The Internet began decades ago as a high-speed data network connecting federally funded supercomputing research sites. Two developments transformed this network in the early 1990s: international agreement on the HyperText Transfer Protocol (http) and HyperText Markup Language (html); and development of "browser" software that translates html files into the formatted words and images we see as Web sites. Today a dizzying array of Web sites is available online.

Organizations can make excellent use of the research possibilities at sites throughout the Web. Certainly there is more and better information available than ever before, and *search engines* make it easy to find both specific sites and sites that might have content that meets your needs. Once you find a useful site, embedded *hypertext* links make it easy to jump from one section to another and find what you are looking for. There are also a great many Web sites of dubious value, and no overarching authority vets Web sites for quality or accuracy. Often the domain name helps to put a site in context: .gov, government; .edu, educational institution; .org, nonprofit organization.

If your nonprofit is considering hosting a Web site (or already has one up and running), take a close look at how the content will meet audience needs and expectations. An important initial consideration is to define the purpose of the Web site: Will it be a placeholder site that provides basic information about the organization, an interactive site with password protection for members and member restricted information and calls to action, or a public site that is interactive and open to all who come to the site. Rather than hosting a public Web site, some organizations operate an *intranet*, for internal use in exchanging files and information.

Public Web sites should contain a strategic mix of what the audiences want to know and what the organization wants to say about itself, its programs, and its services. Remember that a Web site should help meet the communications objectives. How are key audiences likely to use the site, and what do you hope to accomplish? At a minimum, the site should feature complete contact information for the organization (mailing address, phone, e-mail). Some organizations offer content only (articles, research reports, data, images), while others build in more complex layers of interactivity (downloads, quizzes scored online). As with any vehicle, the organization is best served by clean design, plain language, and a structure that is easy to navigate. Be mindful that the more complicated the site, the higher the costs to develop, maintain, and upgrade all the files and related software.

Once the site is up and running, it will be located and indexed by search engines. These software giants run 24 hours a day updating Web addresses and site descriptions—kind of like an Internet phone book. In an increasingly competitive nonprofit environment, the organization can ensure that its site is indexed and described properly by paying careful attention to the *metatags* coded at the top of its Web pages. Metatags tell search engines what information to display when it matches your site to someone's search: *title*, the name of the organization; *description*, a one-liner describing the organization, its work, or its mission; and *keywords*, the words you think target audiences are likely to use in trying to locate your site on the Web.

One of the greatest benefits of Web sites is that they allow people to find the organization. By surfing the Web, people who care about the same issues, programs, and services as the organization can find and become engaged with your nonprofit. As you design your Web site, the level of interactivity for these new audiences should be one of the priorities that the CAT addresses.

Types of Web Sites

Nameplate only	Content delivery	Program delivery
Intranet		Interactive

Benefits of Web Sites

- They allow "seekers" to find you.
- 24-hour availability to clients and audiences.
- Hyperlinks give quick access to desired information.
- It is easy to copy and manipulate text and images on Web sites.
- They can integrate audio and video.
- They automate some line-staff functions (inquiries, responses).
- They can be highly interactive.

Challenges of Web Sites

- They can be expensive to develop and maintain.
- There is uneven access to required technology among audiences.
- Poorly organized or maintained content can do more harm than good.

Rules of the Road: Web Sites

1. The webmaster and communications staff should follow these general guidelines:
- Always include your organization's complete contact information (phone, e-mail, mailing address) on the home page.
- Keep the site simple and well organized. A consistent navigation bar that appears on each page can help people navigate the site.
- Use caution in featuring external links. Web addresses change rapidly, which can result in stale content on the site. To a large extent, adding an external link endorses that site's content, over which the organization has no control.
- As with e-mail addresses, try to choose a Web address that reflects well on the organization. Ask the site host about registering your own domain name.
- Make good use of titles, descriptions, and keyword metatags. Using keywords, do a Net search for your organization. Are search engines finding your Web site and featuring the correct information?
- Gauge the Web site's features to the connection speed of your target audiences. Few people using telephone connections or older modems will have the patience to download a byte-heavy home page.
2. If the organization decides to include elaborate or heavily interactive features, senior management must commit to maintaining and servicing these areas.

- The ease of putting information out on the Web can lead to over-dependence on this vehicle.
- Web sites are essentially passive: people must come to you.
- Keeping information light, layered, and linked.

Guiding Questions

- Have staff members identified all the development and maintenance costs (e.g., equipment, staff, training, time)?
- Do the costs outweigh the benefits in achieving the communications objectives?
- How can the organization use other communications vehicles to promote the Web site?
- Are staff members excited about the application of this vehicle? Will they be willing to learn the new technologies and keep the content up to date?

Strategic Use of Communications Vehicles

The CAT is responsible for pulling all of the communications vehicles together in a manner that best serves each of its communications objectives and all of the targeted audiences. Doing this requires a thorough understanding of the communications audit and the inventory of communications vehicles. As the CAT reviews each of the targeted audiences and the strategies that will be part of the plan, identify gaps in either message or vehicles and determine what additional communications vehicles may be needed.

Guiding Questions

- Which vehicles work in concert with each other to present the message tailored for this target audience? What key message elements are missing?
- Is it possible to modify some of the existing pieces, or do new vehicles need to be developed?
- If additional materials are developed, can they be written in such a way that they can be used with multiple audiences with maximum impact?
- Do any of the strategies contradict each other or impede the possibility of success with targeted audiences?
- Have we considered how the messages respond to the information needs of our audience when they are in each stage of the communications cycle: inform, engage, motivate to act, and maintain? Is there a way to strengthen these message components in any of the selected vehicles?

- Does every vehicle focus on the mission of the organization and the purpose of the communication? Does each include an action step for every audience?

Alternative Media

The organization might also want to consider using other types of vehicles that do not fit neatly into the categories listed. Many of these vehicles— usually considered give-aways or products to sell to raise money for an organization—can give your message added momentum or, at the very least, reinforce it within certain target audience groups. Some ideas might include graffiti, sidewalk art, wearing apparel (T-shirts, hats, jackets, sweat-shirts, etc.), bumper stickers, consumer products (milk cartons, soda cans, grocery bags, etc.), tote bags, buttons, mugs, banners, balloons, and bookmarks. Some more creative ideas might include banner art on Web sites, advertisements in bus stops or on train cars, billboard advertise-ments and the like. Obviously, this category is limited only by the CAT's imagination. Do not let the gimmickry get in the way of your communica-tions strategy, but do not be so wedded to your communications outcomes that you fail to use whimsy when it might serve the organization well.

Building a Comprehensive Portfolio of Communications Vehicles to Support the Communications Objectives

Worksheets 21 through 23 will guide the CAT through an assessment of existing communications vehicles. Worksheet 21 helps the CAT evaluate existing materials and potential strategies to ensure that they meet the needs of multiple audiences. Worksheet 22 is designed to demonstrate how face-to-face, print, audio, video, and electronic media work in concert with each other for maximum benefit with each target audience on each communica-tions objective. Worksheet 23 demonstrates how all the pieces come together to maximum benefit.

Worksheet 21, found at the end of this chapter, can be used to evaluate existing vehicles and strategies.

Worksheet 22, found at the end of this chapter, can be used to plan new vehicles and strategies.

Worksheet 23, found at the end of this chapter, can be used to put it all together.

Worksheet 20 Evaluating Strategic Options

Targeted Audience: _____

Step 1. Review the strategic options under consideration and assign a numeric value (from 1 to 5, with 5 being the highest) for the effectiveness of each strategy against the seven criteria.

  1. *Responsive to audience:* 1 unresponsive, 5 highly responsive
  2. *Appropriate relationship:* 1 inappropriate, 5 builds on our strengths
  3. *Strategy affects perception:* 1 emotional, 5 rational
  4. *Strategy affects message:* 1 no control over message, 5 we control message
  5. *Effort to implement:* 1 draws on our strengths, 5 will tax our capacity
  6. *Cost to implement:* 1 least expensive, 5 most expensive
  7. *Impact on others:* 1 no impact on others, 5 allows us to reach other targeted audiences

Step 2. Decide which strategies are the most likely to give you the desired result with the target audience.
Step 3. Rank order the effective strategies for this target audience and this strategic communications objective.

Strategy	Responsive to audience	Appropriate relationship	Strategy affects perception	Strategy affects message	Effort to implement	Cost to implement	Impact on other audiences	Total	Rank order
1									
2									
3									
4									
5									
6									

Worksheet 21 Evaluate Existing Vehicles and Strategies

Step 1. List existing vehicles used by your organization.
Step 2. Identify priority audiences that could benefit from these vehicles.
Step 3. Verify that each vehicle carries the right message.
Step 4. Verify that the vehicle is effectively reaching the audience.

STEP 1	STEP 2	STEP 3	STEP 4
Vehicles we use	Primary audience	Conveys our message?	Effective at reaching the audience?
Face-to-Face			
1.			
2.			
3.			
Print			
1.			
2.			
3.			
Audio			
1.			
2.			
3.			
Video			
1.			
2.			
3.			

Web site/E-mail			
1.			
2.			
3.			

Which vehicles are effective for reaching target audiences?

Which vehicles need improvement?

What additional vehicles are essential to reach our communication objectives?

Worksheet 22 Plan New Vehicles and Strategies

Communications Objective 1

Target Audience: _____

State Objective: _____

_____

_____

_____

Which vehicles will you use, how will you use them, and why are they good strategic choices?

☐ **Face-to-Face** _____

_____

_____

☐ **Print** _____

_____

_____

☐ **Audio** _____

_____

_____

☐ **Video** _____

_____

_____

☐ **Web site/E-mail** _____

_____

_____

☐ **Other** _____

_____

_____

Worksheet 23 Pull It All Together

Indicate how these vehicles support your strategy for each audience. If possible, indicate where each vehicle supports the others and when they will be used as standalone outreach. Consider how each piece reinforces the persuasive message.

Audience	Face to face	Print	E-mail	Audio	Video	Web site
1.						
2.						
3.						

Step Seven: Ensuring that the Plan Succeeds Measurement and Evaluation

Performance Evaluation

If you don't define your successes, others will discuss your failures.

Performance evaluation is a relatively recent requirement for the communications activities performed by nonprofit organizations. At one time, nonprofits could generate goodwill by reporting on the positive efforts they were making in the community. Now, as budgets tighten and foundations seek to verify the value of the programs they fund, grantees face the challenge of reporting the impact of their efforts. By demonstrating results, organizations reap external benefits through greater community credibility, new funding opportunities, and stronger constituent support.

Evaluation can also benefit an organization internally. Measurement results provide program managers with an opportunity to learn what is working well, enhance program development, and maximize innovation. It also enables programs to respond quickly to change, make midcourse corrections, learn from mistakes, and prevent future errors. As monitoring and evaluation become a routine part of the work culture, the nonprofit will find that this greater awareness of what is going on actually shortens the time for implementing change, enhances the role of all employees and program participants, and stimulates continual internal improvement.

Steps in the Evaluation Process

Task One: Define the audience for and the purpose of the evaluation. Is it an internal review to improve overall project management? Is it an evaluation to be submitted to a funder or governmental agency? Is it part of an annual review with a broad public dissemination? The answers to these questions will help define the structure and approach of the evaluation.

Task Two: Review the goals and measurable objectives. Review the goals and objectives developed at the beginning of the strategic communications planning process. What criteria did the board or the communications action team (CAT) use to define the success of the communications efforts? Did the CAT stay true to that course, or did it make midcourse corrections? Was the CAT successful in defining mechanisms for tracking activities? If not, what records exist of work over the past six months? What monitoring mechanisms can be put in place now to evaluate the impact of work still in process?

Task Three: Develop a review team and a timetable for completion. As in overall project management, it is important to have the people involved in creating, managing, and implementing the project participate in the evaluation team. The CAT should certainly be part of the evaluation process. To the extent possible, program participants and third-party observers should also be given an opportunity to provide input. They may propose measurement standards that those responsible for the communication plan have not considered.

Task Four: Determine the best way to measure whether the objectives were achieved. The review team should also focus on measuring communications impact, not just communications activity. Remember the communications objectives developed at the start of this process; the guiding principle was that everyone who will help execute the plan should have some input in shaping it. The same is true for monitoring and evaluation.

Task Five: Develop a review process for the evaluation report. The process of review and approval is the last opportunity to ensure quality control and to determine how to build commitment for the steps that have been implemented. The CAT needs to determine who will review and respond to the draft.

Concepts that Have Driven the Strategic Communications Process

As the CAT begins the review and evaluation process, it is valuable to review the various communications concepts that have driven the strategic communications plan:

1. *Cycle of communications.* An underlying goal of every communications activity has been the recruitment of new, potentially interested

audiences to join the organization in some way. Equally important has been the desire to engage those who are informed and to get them motivated to act. Finally, we want to retain and continue to involve the base, those who have made a commitment and become involved. Understanding where people fall within the cycle of communications ensures that we give them the information that matches their information needs and we ask them to participate at a level that matches their comfort zone.

2. *Framing issues in concert with public understanding.* Using the framing model, the organization has sought to frame its issues as systemic problems that must be resolved through public policy, community action, individual initiative, or some combination of the three. Evaluating each of these three approaches may suggest where and how the organization addresses new issues in the future. If its greatest strength is in its relationships with public officials, it should initiate more programs in this arena. If working on motivating its base prompts greatest community change, it should identify other opportunities in this arena. If its strength is in individual action, then it should seek opportunities in this arena.

3. *SMART communications objectives.* The organization has developed communications to advance the plan that are Specific, Measurable, Achievable, Realistic, and Time-bound. Knowing what the organization is trying to accomplish will ensure that it can evaluate whether its efforts are being focused in the right place.

4. *Targeted audiences.* By centering its efforts on the active and the aware publics, the organization has focused its communications efforts into those programs and activities that are most likely to generate greater individual and public involvement, attract the attention of public officials, and engage community partners.

5. *Strategies that support the communications objectives.* The organization has selected the best strategies by relying on the seven criteria: audience responsiveness, the organization's relationship with the audience, how the strategy will influence the audience's perceptions, ability to control the message, the effort required to implement, the cost in terms of financial and staff resources, and the potential for replication with other audiences.

6. *Message discipline.* Using the message triangle and other tools to evaluate the words and language used, the nonprofit has developed a strong organization description, selected three or four themes, and designed persuasive messages to tell its story, explain its importance to the target audience, and make specific requests for action.

Measuring Success in Achieving Communications Objectives

Learning whether something worked and, if possible, why it worked is critical to success in the long run. Understanding why a strategy did not achieve the anticipated result is also important for future efforts. As a reminder, objectives must specify:

- Targeted audience to be affected
- Nature of the intended change or action to be taken
- Specific knowledge, attitude, or behavior to be achieved
- Amount of change desired
- Target date for achieving the objective

Tracking Communications Activities

The most basic level of measurement is a simple count that reflects the types of activities that were undertaken (e.g., number of town meetings, of mailings, of volunteers recruited, of press clips received). These measurements, which reflect what the organization did, can be used to demonstrate activities that the nonprofit undertook. At a minimum, the communications plan should include mechanisms for measuring the number of:

- Messages sent
- Activities held
- Messages placed in the media

The overall plan should specify the number of communications activities to take place. Remember, tracking communications *activities* focuses on the process objectives within the plan, the actions that the organization has taken to engage others in advancing its mission.

Measuring Communications Impact

A tougher and more revealing form of measurement is to assess actual impact—the change that occurs in others as a result of the work of the organization. The CAT will need to determine how much effort to expend to measure results that are often much less apparent. Tracking communications *impact* reflects the organization's success in enlisting others to support the nonprofit and its work. This is where community change occurs and the mission of the organization is truly advanced.

Some areas of communications impact that can be measured are the number of people who:

- *Receive* the messages and invitations
- *Attend* activities or *respond* to the messages
- *Learn* the message
- *Change* their opinions or attitudes
- *Behave* in the desired fashion, or who *repeat* desired behaviors

Tracking these numbers allows the CAT to demonstrate that its communications planning process is advancing these measures. Among the factors that can be presented to demonstrate progress, the CAT should include the quality of message presentations (style, format, and packaging); the appropriateness of message content, the organization of information, and the accurate assessment of the audience's level of awareness and information needs.

Techniques that can support efforts to measure impact include readership surveys, focus groups, and interviews with program participants and/or community leaders. Note that the true impact of an organization's communications activities is very hard to measure; even with the best evaluation tools and the most stringent methodologies, it is difficult to isolate the effects of the organization's communications program from other factors that may affect the awareness, knowledge, attitudes, and behaviors of target audiences.

Evaluation Tools

In addition to the internal measurements that were considered during the formation of the communications objectives, external measures can also add to the validity of the evaluation report. Three tools will be presented here: focus groups, clipping services and analysis, and sample surveys.

Focus Groups.   Focus groups allow the organization to test messages at the concept stage as well as to determine how to organize and present information. In a focus group, a trained moderator presents basic information and leads the participants through a series of precise statements to determine how they are responding to the information presented. Focus groups are a useful tool when an organization wants to know how members of a key audience perceive the organization and its work. Group participants can discuss issues of importance to the organization, to inform it about their values and attitudes, and to share their response to various strategic options under consideration. Once messages have been tested and reformulated, organizations with additional resources may want to conduct a quantitative survey with a larger sample of the target audience to measure the reaction to various messages. Results from focus groups cannot—and should not—be extrapolated to the larger population.

Clipping Services and Analysis.   Clipping services and analysis requires the systematic collection of clippings, preferably both print and electronic media. Clipping service firms can conduct this research, or interns can compile the clippings. It is important to remember to include trade and other specialized media; these are sources where important target audiences get their information. There are several ways to analyze clips:

- Volume of coverage—how much was written or how many minutes of air time
- Messages sent versus messages placed—the number of press releases, phone calls, interviews, and so on that resulted in coverage
- How often the coverage accurately reflected the message, the organization, and the message frame

The evaluation of these data should assess how much coverage was achieved in each media outlet (by publication, radio, or television) to determine which audiences were reached and how many times they were exposed to the message. This is accomplished by merging the data from the clipping analysis with the data from secondary sources—audience characteristics and circulation/TV radio ratings or audience share—which can be obtained directly from the media outlet. By combining these two sets of data, an organization can begin to understand how often the general public is receiving its messages.

In addition, the organization should evaluate the content of the coverage: Is the story positive, neutral, or negative? What specific frames were featured? Were the organization's frame, name, and messages prominently featured in the story? Was the coverage news, editorial, letter to the editor, feature story, or something else?

Note that this evaluation does not directly address the impact of the organization's strategic communications work. Rather, it indicates how the organization's story is being conveyed to the public by the media. Several other factors will influence how the story is actually received by the target audience.

Sampling Surveys.   Online surveys are a quick and easy way for the organization to connect with those who regularly visit its Web site. Sampling surveys have become easier to conduct with the advent of listservs and improvements in online technology. Online surveys provide an opportunity to ask active users of the site to self-select to provide quick feedback. Readily available options include readership surveys sent at the end of an e-newsletter, Survey Monkey, and online questionnaires. The value of these surveys is that the respondents are the target, audience for the communications activity; the disadvantage is that those who respond are most likely to be active support-ers and already engaged in the work of the organization.

Guiding Questions

- What type of feedback do we need to assess the impact of our communications efforts?
- What can we measure that would indicate whether our activities are getting us closer to achieving our communications objectives?
- Are we reaching our target audiences? Are they taking the desired actions?
- Are we meeting our target dates? Are we ahead of our timetable?
- What efforts are generating the greatest return on investment?
- Aside from questionnaires, what nontraditional ways might we use to measure changes in opinions, attitudes, and behaviors?

Monitoring the Progress on Communications Objectives

Worksheet 24 will assist the CAT in determining measurable actions for evaluating process goals and measurable impacts for evaluating whether target audiences move along the cycle of communications. The form can be a useful tool for indicating the need for midcourse corrections.

Worksheet 24, found at the end of this chapter, can be used to help the CAT determine measurable outcomes for its commu-nications activities and impact.

Finalize the Report

In developing the final report, make sure that the CAT continues to involve all stakeholders and program participants in the design, data collection, and analysis activities of the evaluation. The process will proceed more smoothly if the evaluation effort can position participants as problem solvers and not as critics seeking to highlight problems.

In presenting its findings, the CAT should make sure to present positive findings first, using qualitative as well as quantitative data. Anecdotal stories will put a human face on successes and help your stakeholders understand that the value of the strategic communications plan extends beyond its financial or administrative successes. Frame the negative findings in the context of lessons learned and opportunities for further program change and growth. Do not attempt to cover up elements of the project that have not worked as anticipated. Highlight what was learned from those elements and steps that have been taken to improve or adjust expectations.

Rules of the Road: Keys to Successful Evaluations

1. The CAT should build evaluation components into the initial communications plan design.

2. The CAT establishes concise, measurable objectives that demonstrate communications *impact*, not just communications *activities*.

3. The CAT will want to involve program managers as part of the review team and convene them in that capacity from the beginning of the project, and at regular interviews, to provide input into the final report and presentations. Incorporate routine reviews of what is working and what needs improvement into program management meetings.

4. The CAT will also want to involve stakeholders and program participants in the design, data collection, and analysis activities of the evaluation.

5. The CAT should tailor the evaluation to the target audience and consider other potential audiences that would be interested in the results.

6. The CAT can enrich the quality of the evaluation by including both qualitative and quantitative data that insert a ``human face'' into the evaluation wherever possible.

Worksheet 24   Develop Outcome Measures

Reexamine the communications objectives you created for Worksheet 13. List three measurable activities and three measurable impacts. If necessary, revise the communications objective to be sure you are measuring both activities and impact.

Communications Objective 1

Activities to Measure:

1. _____
2. _____
3. _____

Impacts to Measure:

1. _____
2. _____
3. _____

State or revise the communications objective to demonstrate impact:

_____
_____
_____
_____

Communications Objective 2

Activities to Measure:

1. _____
2. _____
3. _____

Impacts to Measure:

1. _____
2. _____
3. _____

State or revise the communications objective to demonstrate impact:

_____
_____
_____
_____

10

Pulling It All Together
Creating the Plan

Building the Communications Plan

Now that all the research, analysis, and brainstorming have been done, it is time to bring all the pieces together and build the communications plan. All the possible strategies that have been considered will now be sorted through and prioritized. By bringing together all these strands—which strategies to implement; when each will happen; what it will take to make it happen; and who will be responsible for various tasks, strategies, and objectives—the communications action team (CAT) will create a road map for the organization's communications. Although everyone's plans will look different on paper—some people prefer text while others prefer charts and lists—the plan will include the components listed next.

As it has constructed the plan, the CAT has looked at the organization from the broadest view and in minute detail. This comprehensive assessment will contribute to the overall success of the plan. As a reminder, here are the seven steps of the strategic communications process.

1. Preparing to plan by reviewing the mission, program goals, and other planning documents.
2. A situation analysis, internal and external, outlining the environment in which your organization works and developing the SWOT analysis.
3. Target and research audiences (prioritized from most important to least important) for each communications objective, including a summary of their connection to the organization and its issues.
4. Communications objectives that are SMART.
5. Targeted messages for each objective, modified to fit each audience.
6. Strategies and the specific vehicles to implement those strategies. This is based on an action plan that includes:

- Timeline and task list for each vehicle, identifying the individuals responsible for each task and strategy
- Estimated budget, identifying needed funding and sources (e.g., budget reallocation, new funding, in-kind contributions)
- Calendar of current organizational activities, holidays and local events, and related activities from other organizations that will help manage the plan

  7. A plan for data collection, monitoring, and evaluation.

Having brainstormed and prioritized possible strategies and vehicles for each audience, the CAT needs to think through the "when and where" of the plan. The strategies the organization decides to pursue must be organized in a way that will fulfill the communications objectives and create new momentum for the issues, initiatives, programs, and so forth. At the same time, the plan must be integrated into existing organizational activities and external events. The plan is a series of actions that moves the organization and its audiences toward the realization of program goals and advancing the nonprofit's mission. It will spell out the communications route the organization staff needs to follow, one day at a time. The plan, although written down, will be a "living" document that changes and grows, always responding to new opportunities, new challenges, and new options.

Putting It All Together

Begin by developing a calendar to track organizational and relevant external activities, holidays, commemorative events, and the like. On this calendar, note scheduled organizational and communications projects.

In tandem with the organizational calendar, complete a planning sheet for each of the priority audiences that clearly state each communications objectives. The planning sheet should include what you know (or need to find out) about each audience, the targeted messages (tested or untested), and a prioritized list of strategies and vehicles to move this audience toward the objective(s).

Select "target dates" for each strategy—the day(s) on which the audience will experience or receive the communication. A simple example is a quarterly mailing. On the planning sheet, note the date of the mailing and, more important, the date the audience should receive the mailing. Use the same approach for each action alert, e-mail update, and press release. When the target audience is an outreach partner such as the press or legislative staff, the first target date should be when it receives the communication; the second target date should be the approximate time an action will be taken on the communication. For example, when the target audience is the press, the first target date is the date that members of the press should receive the press release; the second target date is the day the story might be expected to run.

These target dates will also help the CAT decide when to establish a follow-up date to communicate again with that particular target audience. The CAT can determine the frequency of the organization's communication with a particular audience, which will help it track how often that audience has been exposed to communications from the nonprofit.

As the various strategies come together for a single audience group, consider:

- How will this communications schedule feel to this target audience?
- How will they experience it?
- Over time, will these efforts create the necessary momentum and move this particular audience toward doing what the organization needs them to do in order to achieve the communications objective?

Once the strategies are written down with appropriate target dates set on the calendar, work backward to fill in the various tasks that must be done in order to implement each strategy. For example, if the organization wants to use a monthly newsletter to keep its volunteers informed, the various tasks involved—writing and researching the articles, gathering photos and graphics, layout, proofreading, printing, getting the mailing list to the mail house—should all be plotted on a timeline with the name of the person responsible and an estimated time allotment for how long each step will take.

A newsletter is a relatively simple, straightforward strategy that illustrates the value of identifying tasks and establishing a timeline. Most communications campaigns are complex, and breaking them down into their component parts becomes even more essential.

After the CAT has plotted a six-month strategy for a single audience group, repeat the process with each additional audience group. Detail each step and mark the dates on the staff calendar. Doing so will help the CAT determine the organization's breaking point, or communications-tolerance level. In addition, by slicing and dicing the timeline, the CAT can pull together detailed staff and volunteer task lists with deadlines, deliverables, and responsibilities. The manager of the communications plan can use these tools to ensure that all the work is getting done in a timely fashion, monitor progress, revise where necessary, and determine whether appropriate measures and data collection is occurring.

Once all of the strategies have been compiled, the CAT should look at the overall plan and evaluate the scope of work that has been developed. As it considers priorities for the six month timeframe, it should consider the following points to ensure that the plan, as conceived, can actually be completed.

Guiding Questions

- What is actually doable?
- Are we maximizing the impact of what we plan to do by coordinating adequate follow-up?
- Is the combination of all these strategies affordable?
- Is enough time available to do everything?
- Do we have the staff expertise to handle this, or will we need to bring in someone to help us complete these tasks?
- Do various strategies work together for more than one audience group?
- Do they overlap unnecessarily?
- Can two or more strategies be combined without adversely affecting various audience groups?
- Do any of the messages or strategies contradict or hinder each other?
- If we cannot do it all, which strategies can we cut and still reach our goals?

Creating Organizational Ownership

There has to be a compelling reason for an organization to commit its resources to a new approach. The strategic communications planning process may be a new model for your board, staff, consultants, and activists. Building support for a new approach and the accompanying workload may be the first hurdle to a successful communications effort—and the only way for a communications plan to be successful is if it has 100% buy-in from the entire organization, especially if its programs rely heavily on volunteers.

Although it is not necessary for everyone to understand all the details and the reasons why one strategy was chosen over another, it is important that everyone involved see the connection between the communications plan and the organization's mission and goals. Everyone will need to know the organization's messages in order to communicate them in both professional and personal situations. When everyone in an organization is "on message," the message is communicated beyond the organization in an informal way. Having everyone connected with an organization on message reinforces its impact in both structured and informal settings.

There are many ways to create buy-in for the organization's communications efforts. The first is to think of internal constituencies as audiences and develop messages that will persuade them of the plan's importance.

Although everyone connected with an organization may have its best interests at heart, depending on their roles, different people may define the nonprofit's "best interests" differently. For example, a financial officer may be convinced by a message that stresses communications as a way to leverage existing resources; a program director may be persuaded only by a message that highlights the connection between communications and the organization's program goals, regardless of the cost.

Whose Buy-In Will You Need?

Executive director	Board of directors
Senior management	Line staff
Program staff	Administrative staff
Financial director	Information management staff
Volunteers	

Messages to Support the Communications Plan

The language used to persuade internal constituencies of the importance of practicing strategic communications must resonate with their concerns. It is no less important than the language that has been developed for all other target audiences. It must be designed to tell them about the plan, why it is important to their work at the organization, and what they can do to support the promotion and implementation of the plan. The CAT should spend time developing message triangles addressed to the board, senior management, program staff, and volunteers.

What It Is	Why It Is Important	What Should I Do?
shared vision	revenue	actively contribute
strategic	strengthen organization	learn about it
tool	job security	support it
plan for talking to people	pride in organization	help out
measure of success	edge over competition	put it on the agenda
social change	improve public perception	help reallocate $
window to what we do	more clients, donors, volunteers	don't get in the way
reposition the organization	reframe the issue	lend us your credibility

When tweaking the messages to address the unique perspectives of the various individuals and groups from whom the CAT will need buy-in for the communications plan, always reinforce the idea that "communicating strategically will strengthen the organization, maximize our investment of time, and have a positive impact on our program goals." Many staff members consider participating in interdepartmental teams or thinking outside the box as opportunities to give some of their own imagination and ingenuity back to the organization.

Listening is another component of any buy-in strategy—not to debate a point that is made but rather to emphasize that everyone's ideas are valuable and that the process is an open one. Indeed, listening carefully to what people say will help the CAT assess the extent of staff and volunteer commitment to the communications plan. In addition, hearing their concerns may help the CAT to anticipate potential roadblocks and respond to them before they become problems—which, in the long run, will make the end result stronger and more representative of the entire organization. Remember that the board, senior management, staff, and volunteers also share a commitment to the organization's mission and success.

Several strategies that might be used to create buy-in are suggested next. Obviously, any strategy should be tailored to each organizational culture and reflect the communication preferences of the individual with whom you are communicating. Decide what strategy to use based on previous successes used to build teams, create consensus, develop strategic plans, or launch new program initiatives. Use these to model the best buy-in strategies.

Tips for Building Support

The strategic communications planning process should be considered a communications strategy with appropriate messages and vehicles to ensure its success. The chief executive, the board chair, the CAT, members of the evaluation team and others should all consider communications opportunities for promoting the plan and its many contributions to the nonprofit.

1. Early in the process, the chief executive should put the strategic communications plan on the agenda at a senior management meeting. Work through a condensed version of the seven-step process. Encourage active participation, and use the various questions throughout this communications manual as a starting point for discussion. Focus in particular on the situation analysis, communications

objectives, audience characteristics, and message development—the foundation for any communications plan. Elicit management's thoughts on evaluation criteria—for example, what results would convince them that the communications effort was successful and worth the organization's investment of time and money?

2. The CAT should ask program staff what their goals are for the year. Clarify these goals and make sure they are measurable, without linking them to communications at the outset. Explain how the communications objectives are an integral part of their program goals and that the plan will help the staff achieve success on their program goals.

3. The CAT can invite program staff to participate in a session on message development and on the audit review of communications materials. Understanding how the process works will prepare staff to accept the findings and recommendations. These are opportunities to describe how an important issue is currently positioned and how that affects program objectives and organizational success.

4. The CAT can hold meetings with line staff members to present the organization's objectives, audiences, and draft messages. Ask for their impressions and feedback. Engage all of the nonprofit's staff members to create ownership of the process and to help ensure that everyone is on board. Staff members should understand that they are communicators for the organization and its issues. By "singing from the same hymn book," everyone reinforces the organization's vision and long-term goals.

5. The chief executive and the CAT should conduct a brief presentation for the organization's board of directors, summarizing the communications planning process and the results of the senior staff meeting. If helpful, invite a consultant or volunteer who has experience in communications to attend the meeting. Make the case for a communications plan by discussing the objectives to be addressed and the resources needed. Encourage questions, comments, and ideas. To encourage staff confidence in the plan, it is vital that the board of directors understands and commits to the communications effort early.

6. The CAT can recommend that staff actively recruit volunteers who understand the importance of communications or have experience in the field. They can form a committee and monitor issues in the media, help create messages, suggest evaluation criteria, and assess results. This type of volunteer effort will help validate your communications efforts within the larger organizational structure and contribute the time and energy needed to get the work done.

7. The CAT should regularly promote its work possibly writing a regular column in the organization's newsletter to update staff and volunteers about the communications plan and its impact. Feature names of staff and/or volunteers who have helped, recognizing their work and reinforcing the shared ownership of the communications effort.

8. It is the CAT's responsibility to regularly communicate to the entire organization—staff and volunteers—the reasons for including a communications component in the overall program goals and how communications objectives have helped advance the organization.

9. The CAT should keep staff, board members, and volunteers informed (at least monthly) of the current messages. Provide them with talking points so they know how to frame issues in a way that maximizes the facts through analogy or comparison, uses emotional language, and recognizes the power of storytelling (especially the human, real-life implications of the work of the organization).

Once a communications plan becomes part of the organization's culture, it will become indispensable and part of everyday organizational life. Having people who are aware of the organization's communications plan and who are committed to getting the messages out in both their professional and their personal lives means that the plan—and the mission—will become a matter of fact.

A final benefit of working to achieve organizational buy-in is to ensure that the plan will actually be implemented; many people will be intent on seeing it happen.

Building the Case for Sustainable Capacity

Increasingly, funders are asking nonprofit organizations to demonstrate their case for survival, not just in economic terms but in terms of relevance and performance. *Sustainability* means that an organization has taken steps to address areas that are essential to ensure long-term viability. Guiding questions that can help build the case statement on sustainability follow. As the CAT plans for the future, it should keep these questions on the table. Remember that as the organization's programs evolve, so will its responses and actions. Like the strategic communications plan, the organization's capacity for sustainable programs and activities is dynamic and ever changing.

Essential Elements for Sustainability[1]

Clear vision	Solid financial footing	Technology
Strong leadership	Evaluation	Collaboration
Organizational development	Communications	Advocacy

Clear Vision

- Does the organization have a clear mission, guided by a clear set of values, embraced by all?
- Does the organization have a shared vision of where it is headed, with a strategic plan setting forth goals and strategies to be pursued over the next several years?
- Does the organization have a clear sense of what differentiates it from others that provide similar programs and services?

Strong Leadership

- Is the board fully engaged and supportive of the organization? Are there board committees that oversee policy and support the organizations operations?
- Is the board representative of all the stakeholders served by the organization? Are the requisite leadership skills and experience represented on the board?
- Does the board have a leadership succession plan that is not overly reliant on a few individuals? Is there a board development committee that continually educates members and ensures involvement in board activities?
- Does the organization rely on a strong executive director, or is there an effective senior leadership team to ensure continuity and breadth of capabilities? Is there a clear plan of succession behind the executive director and other key leadership positions?

Organizational Development

- Has the organization assessed its administrative processes, programs, human resources, infrastructure, and development efforts?

---

[1]Profiles in Organizational Effectiveness for Nonprofits: Improving the Lives of Children, Youth and Families in Kansas City. (Ewing Marion Kauffman Foundation, Kansas City MO, 2001), page 1.

- What are the core strengths of the organization on which future success can be built? Are there particular weaknesses that should be addressed?
- Has the organization assessed the forces for change in the external environment (demographic, economic, political, technological, social) that may affect it?
- What are the primary opportunities facing the organization? What are the primary threats?
- Does the nonprofit seek to be a learning organization in which knowledge is shared, creativity is encouraged, and management of change is approached with enthusiasm?
- Are staff roles clearly understood, with performance expectations for everyone?
- Does the organization recruit and develop the best and brightest people to its staff? Are staff members compensated adequately and acknowledged for their performance? Are there opportunities for professional development for all staff members?

Solid Financial Footing

At a minimum, it is essential that organizations be able to answer "yes" to these questions:
- Does the organization have diverse funding sources? Is it not overly dependent on a single funding source?
- Is there mutual respect, knowledge, and integrity between the organization and its funders? Does the nonprofit communicate with its major funders regularly to address fiscal issues or challenges?
- Does the organization attract, create, and sustain sufficient new resources by continually seeking potential funding sources?
- Are appropriate financial controls established and followed within the organization?
- Do independent auditors conduct financial audits and reviews at regular intervals?
- Are financial crises managed or averted?
- Has the organization established a reserve fund sufficient to cover operating expenses for a planned period?
- Does the organization have a documented fund-development plan? If not, does it have an experienced fund-development expert on staff, or as an outside resource, to focus on the development and execution of such a plan?
- Does the organization have clear fund-development goals for individual giving? Corporate giving? Major gifts/planned giving? Special events? Grants?

- If the organization is supported by an endowment, what proportion of the annual operating budget is funded from annual proceeds of the endowment?
- What is the organization's capacity to generate earned income from existing programs, services, facilities, or other sources? Has it identified entrepreneurial strategies for generating additional revenues?
- How effective is the organization in setting budgets and managing them? Are program costs and revenues separately identified and managed? Is the management of cash flow a challenge for the organization?

Evaluation

- Are objective performance measures established for each of the top-priority strategies (critical success factors) for the organization? Are timetables for implementation established with reasonable deadlines?
- Do the executive director and all senior staff have clear performance standards with outcome measures? Is compensation for senior staff based on performance measures?

Communications

- Has the organization identified the audiences with whom it must communicate in order to be successful? Does it understand each audience?
- Is the organization clear about what it wants each audience to do? Does the organization have clear communications objectives for each audience?
- Does the organization communicate clear messages to each of its audiences while maintaining an appropriate overall message and image (brand)?
- What communications vehicles (face-to-face, print, e-mail, audio, video, Web site) is it using to reach each target audience? How does the organization measure the effectiveness of each vehicle?

Technology

- Does the organization have a well-defined technology plan that identifies how technology will support its mission?
- Has the organization planned for future technology needs and developed specifications for hardware, software, staffing, and training? Does the organization have a schedule for implementing technology projects?
- Does the organization have multiyear budgets for meeting its technology needs, including hardware, software, staffing, and training?

- Has the organization identified resources in the community to help it identify and plan for its technology needs?

Collaboration

Within the nonprofit world, it is almost impossible to do it alone. The most effective organizations have learned to pool their resources with others for the common good of the community. Effective partnering means recognizing and capitalizing on the unique skills and resources of others to maximize your own strengths.

- Has the organization identified key partners that share its mission and vision?
- Does the organization work closely with other nonprofits and private enterprises to expand its ability to realize its mission and gain access to resources that are not available within?
- Has the organization defined the characteristics of desirable partnerships and identified ways that collaboration can provide mutual benefits?
- Does the organization have a plan of action for collaborations, with specific roles, responsibilities, and timelines defined?

Advocacy

Nonprofits often fail to ask for the support of their allies to advance their mission and ensure sustainability. Advocates can help the nonprofit organization build public awareness, connect with key policy makers and decision makers, and raise essential public and private resources.

- Has the organization identified allies who can advocate for its programs, determining which ones have influential connections that can be tapped?
- Has the organization educated its advocates about the key messages and timetables and defined advocates' role in advancing the strategic communications plan?

Money: If It Is a Good Idea, You Can Sell It

Implementing the communications plan should be a shared responsibility, beginning with formation of the CAT. The CAT should be responsible for ensuring that the communications strategies are cost-effective and achieve the desired results. If reallocating existing money does not cover the cost of the plan, the CAT should determine how to raise money from outside sources. (Obviously, if an organization has a fundraising staff or a board development committee, individuals from those groups probably would take the lead in raising these funds.)

Like everything else, the key to raising the necessary financial support for the communications plan is to develop messages that will move the audience—in this case grant makers, agency officials, or individual donors— to act. Most grant makers—and government agencies—want organizations to disseminate information about their programs or results. Show how these communications efforts connect to the organization's mission and program goals. Many acknowledge the importance of outreach to target populations. Funders want organizations to influence public policy as well as human behavior, attitudes, and opinions. In order to achieve these outcomes, an organization must practice strategic communications—and that takes money. Build your communications expenses into the proposals submitted to raise money for your programs.

Rules of the Road: Creating Buy-In

The communications plan is an integral part of the success of the organization and its programs.

It has a direct effect on the organization's ability to serve its clients and the community.

The cost of implementing the plan must be seamlessly woven into grant proposals.

Learn to make the strongest case to grant makers, business leaders, and individual donors. Now that the CAT understands the critical connection between the organization's goals, its audiences, and the resulting communications objectives, learn how to explain communications to funders in a way that focuses on the program and not on "making a video" or "publishing a newsletter." Do not be afraid to say: "These communications activities are crucial to our program's success, and we need to be able to do this to accomplish our program goals."

In the midst of implementing your organization's communications plan, the CAT should take advantage of opportunities that arise to raise additional support for its efforts. For example, if the organization (or its issue) is featured in the media, consider piggybacking a targeted direct-mail campaign to those audiences most likely to have been exposed to that media. The mailing does not have to be fancy—a letter from the chief executive, board president, or spokesperson, along with a clean copy of the clipping, can be sent to high-dollar donors, business leaders, and others to solicit additional financial support.

Income-Producing Possibilities

Knowledge is valuable, and the products that result from that knowledge are also valuable. Many nonprofit organizations believe that their mission is to educate targeted audiences to create social change, and have tended to give away the information and knowledge they produce. Nevertheless, the organization may want to explore whether to charge secondary audiences for certain knowledge products that it currently gives away. If the organization decides to charge for information that it produces, this strategy must be built into your communications plan—how the material should be packaged, what messages should be developed to demonstrate value for investment, and where third-party endorsements of the material can be found. Even something as simple as charging for the cost of printing and distribution can mean the organization is able to produce an extra product or two.

In-Kind Contributions

Compile a list of nonfinancial contributions that the CAT could use to implement the strategies in the plan (e.g., equipment, professional services, printing, graphic design, postage, video editing and dubbing). Brainstorm with members of the staff, current vendors, or a small pool of volunteers about businesses, corporations, large-membership organizations, and even public institutions that might be able to contribute this type of support. Local colleges and universities may be interested in contributing student projects, such as video production, designing brochures and templates, or even conducting part of the assessment itself.

Assign each member of the CAT several contacts to solicit for non-financial support. Rehearse the CAT's message—why implementing this strategy is important to the success of the organization's program and why that program is critical to the welfare of the community. It may also be useful to note any tangible or intangible benefit for the sponsor. For example, a sponsor could receive free publicity if its assistance is noted in information the nonprofit distributes.

One word of caution about accepting in-kind contributions: Always retain final approval of the work or service being contributed. For example, a brochure that is beautifully designed but inaccurately reflects the organization's mission or programs is not worth the contribution and can, in fact, cause confusion or problems as well as the loss of goodwill on both sides.

Before finalizing and launching any communications plan, ensure that these four elements are in place:

1. Organizational buy-in
2. Expertise
3. Time
4. Money

These four elements are critical to the success of the strategic communications plan and the impact it will have on your organization, your programs, and the community you serve.

Strategic Communications Plan Template

Mission Statement

20- to 25-Word Organization Description

Program Goals

Strategic Communications Plan

Step One
Conduct a Situation Analysis

A. Examine the External Environment

Demographic Force: Who are the primary groups that benefit from the organization? Has there been a shift or change in the populations or the makeup of the communities you serve? If yes, what does that mean? If no, is that cause for alarm?

Economic Forces: What are the sources of revenue for the organization? Is the financial base sufficiently diversified? How do donors perceive the organization, and what does that mean for its financial future (consider government funding, foundations, and corporate contributors)? Is the economy shifting in ways that will cause a growth or a decline in demand for services from the populations we serve?

Technological Forces: What are the latest trends in business technology that might allow the organization to be more effective? What are the latest products or trends in online technology that could impact the work: program development, technical assistance, volunteer recruitment, training, education, and so on? How will recent trends impact the organization? Does the organization need to improve its technology to create better products, improve services, and/or conduct more cost-effective advocacy efforts?

Political Forces: How do current political priorities influence the organization and its work? What will be on the national, local, and state political agenda this year? Could it affect the organization or the populations it serves? If the winds blow our way, what can we expect? If they go against us, what is the worst that can happen? Is there something we are **not** seeing?

Social Forces: What social or cultural trends are occurring in the community, in the state, in the nation? What does this mean for the organization and its work? What social or cultural values are embraced by the constituents that we serve? Have these values changed recently? If so, why? Does that impact the organization's relationship to its constituents? What is the mood of the nation? the community? What is the latest fear in society? What is the latest demand? What is the latest hope or solution being talked about? How could these fears, demands, and hopes impact the organization and its work?

B. Examine the Internal Environment

Management Objectives: Is there a strategic plan that guides the work of the organization? Are there clear management objectives? Are staff members aware of the management objectives of the organization and what that means for their job performance? How do they relate to program objectives? Has the organization defined what each management objective means and why it is important for the organization's success? Are there mechanisms for staff input or feedback?

Human Resources: What expertise does the staff have? What knowledge base resides in the staff? Do we provide training for staff? Do we have staff expertise in all the areas on which the organization is focused? Do we have too many or not enough volunteers for the programs that require volunteer involvement? What additional staffing do we require?

Financial Resources: Is the organization on sound financial footing? Do its financial resources covering existing activities? Does the organization pay its expenses in a timely manner? Does the organization have a reserve fund? Does the organization have a core group of supporters and donors? Does this base need to be expanded? diversified?

Physical Infrastructure: Does the organization have enough workspace for staff, consultants, and temporary workers? Is the space conducive to teamwork? Are there adequate light, air, and heat? Can people have a private conversation if they need to? Is the neighborhood safe for staff working odd hours? Is there room to expand if the organization takes on new programs?

Technology Infrastructure: Do people have adequate computers and software to perform their jobs? Does the telephone system meet the needs of the organization? Are there other special equipment needs that should be addressed?

How will these factors influence the implementation of our strategic communications plan?

C. Strengths, Weaknesses, Opportunities, Threats

What are our strengths?

What are our weaknesses?

What opportunities exist in the next 18 months?

What threats exist in the next 18 months?

D. Analyze Strengths, Weaknesses, Opportunities, Threats

	Opportunities	Threats
Strengths		
Weaknesses		

Unique opportunity for the next six months:

-
-
-
-

Challenge to address in the next six months:

-

Step Two
Connect with Your Audience

A. Audience Identification

Step 1. Review the following list and rate each audience in terms of its importance to your work (somewhat important, critically important, or not applicable).

Step 2. Decide whether you have been effective or not effective at reaching out to them.

Step 3. Rank the five most critical audiences for this planning process. Check the appropriate boxes.

Category	Step 1			Step 2		Step 3
	N/A	Somewhat Important	Critical	Not Effective	Effective	Rank the Top 5
Colleagues at other organizations						
Organizations with similar program interests and values or with whom we partner						
Organizations that oppose our work						
Activists/advocates (against us)						
Clients						
Activists/advocates (for us)						
Board members						
Volunteers						
Staff						
Private foundations						
Corporate foundations						

Donors				
Community leaders				
Community groups				
Church groups				
Government officials/policy makers				
Nongovernment policy makers				
Parents				
Educators/teachers				
Corporations—senior managers				
Small business owners				
Young people				
Health care providers				
Social service agencies				
Academic or trade press				
National press				
State and local reporters, editors, media outlets, specific programs				
Other audience(s) not on this list:				

B. Audience Profile

Audience _____

1. Describe your audience: What are their concerns? What characteristics of your audience are important to your organization (e.g., their education levels, income levels; family size, health issues)?

2. Why are they important to you?

3. Why should your audience care about your organization and its issues?

4. What do you want from this audience?

5. How does this audience receive information?

6. Are there particular individuals who have credibility or power over the target audience? What are their names?

7. Are there other individuals that can help you better reach this target audience? Who?

C. Select Priority Audiences

Review the previous list and select five groups that you will focus on for your strategic communications plan. Indicate how they are important to your work and the desired action you would like them to take.

Audience	Why Are They Important to Us?	Desired Action
EXAMPLE: NPO	Provides coordination with similar projects around our mission. Identifies resource needs and develops standard language on our issue.	How to work together and when we can work alone.
1.		
2.		
3.		
4.		
5.		

Step Three
Communications Objectives

Remember that communications objectives focus on changing specific knowledge, attitudes, or behaviors in the audience. Communications objectives have action verbs (e.g., educate, teach, inform, provide, conduct, enlist, mobilize, discuss, promote, build consensus).

Communications Objective 1

Target Audience:

Select One: ☐ Inform   ☐ Engage   ☐ Motivate   ☐ Maintain

Desired Action:

Target Date:

State Objective:

Communications Objective 2

Target Audience:

Select One: ☐ Inform   ☐ Engage   ☐ Motivate   ☐ Maintain

Desired Action:

Target Date:

State Objective:

Apply the **SMART** test. Are your communications objectives:

☐ Smart?   ☐ Measurable?   ☐ Appropriate?   ☐ Realistic?   ☐ Time-bound?

Communications Objective 3

Target Audience:

Select One: ☐ Inform   ☐ Engage   ☐ Motivate   ☐ Maintain

Desired Action:

Target Date:

State Objective:

Communications Objective 4

Target Audience:

Select One: ☐ Inform   ☐ Engage   ☐ Motivate   ☐ Maintain

Desired Action:

Target Date:

State Objective:

Apply the **SMART** test. Are your communications objectives:

☐ Smart?   ☐ **Measurable?**   ☐ **Appropriate?**   ☐ **Realistic?**   ☐ **Time-bound?**

Communications Objective 5

Target Audience:

Select One: ☐ Inform   ☐ Engage   ☐ Motivate   ☐ Maintain

Desired Action:

Target Date:

State Objective:

Communications Objective 6

Target Audience:

Select One: ☐ Inform   ☐ Engage   ☐ Motivate   ☐ Maintain

Desired Action:

Target Date:

State Objective:

Apply the **SMART** test. Are your communications objectives:

☐ Smart?   ☐ Measurable?   ☐ Appropriate?   ☐ Realistic?   ☐ Time-bound?

Step Four
Tailor Messages

A. Persuasive Messages

Create a message for each of your priority audiences. It should have three parts. It should identify the issue and desired change, make it relevant to the audience, and provide an action step that the audience can take. Write your message as a complete sentence or two. Try to use the most persuasive language and use the word "you" at least once.

Target Audience: _____

Desired Change: _____

```
                    /\
                   /  \
                  /    \
                 /      \
         Issue  /        \  Why Should Your
               /          \  Audience Care
              /            \
             /              \
            /_____\

        What You Want Your Audience
           to Do, Think, or Feel
```

Part 1 (Issue)

Part 2 (Why Should Your Audience Care)

Part 3 (What You Want Your Audience to Do, Think, or Feel)

> Now write a message combining all 3 parts as if you are talking to the audience.

Persuasive Messages

Create a message for each of your priority audiences. It should have three parts. It should identify the issue and desired change, make it relevant to the audience, and provide an action step that the audience can take. Write your message as a complete sentence or two. Try to use the most persuasive language and use the word "you" at least once.

Target Audience: _____

Desired Change: _____

```
                    /\
                   /  \
                  /    \
                 /      \
        Issue   /        \   Why Should Your
               /          \  Audience Care
              /            \
             /              \
            /_____\
       What You Want Your Audience
         to Do, Think, or Feel
```

Part 1 (Issue)

Part 2 (Why Should Your Audience Care)

Part 3 (What You Want Your Audience to Do, Think, or Feel)

Now write a message combining all 3 parts as if you are talking to the audience.

B. Put a Human Face on the Work

Select an anecdote that puts a "human face" on the work that you do.

Select a second anecdote that puts a "human face" on the work that you do.

What do these anecdotes say about the work that you do? What emotions are they likely to trigger with your target audience? Are there any privacy concerns or other issues that should be addressed before you use these anecdotes?

Step Five
Develop Strategies and Vehicles

A. Evaluate Strategic Options

Targeted Audience: _____

Step 1. Review the strategic options under consideration and assign a numeric value (from 1 to 5, with 5 being the highest) for the effectiveness of each strategy against the seven criteria.

1. Responsive to Audience: 1 unresponsive, 5 highly responsive
2. Appropriate Relationship: 1 inappropriate, 5 builds on our strengths
3. Strategy Affects Perception: 1 emotional, 5 rational
4. Strategy Affects Message: 1 no control over message, 5 we control message
5. Effort to Implement: 1 draws on our strengths, 5 will tax our capacity
6. Cost to Implement: 1 least expensive, 5 most expensive
7. Impact on Others: 1 no impact on others, 5 allows us to reach other targeted audiences

Step 2. Decide which strategies are the most likely to give you the desired result with the target audience.

Step 3. Rank order the effective strategies for this target audience and this strategic communications objective.

Strategy	Responsive to audience	Appropriate relationship	Strategy affects perception	Strategy affects message	Effort to implement	Cost to implement	Impact on other audiences	Total	Rank order

Are all of these strategies designed to work in concert with each other and to be mutually reinforcing?

B. Evaluate Existing Vehicles and Strategies

Step 1. List existing vehicles used by your organization.
Step 2. Identify priority audiences that could benefit from these vehicles.
Step 3. Verify that each vehicle carries the right message.
Step 4. Verify that the vehicle is effectively reaching the audience.

Step 1	Step 2	Step 3	Step 4
Vehicles we use	Primary audience	Conveys our message?	Effective at reaching the audience?
Face-to-Face			
Print			
Audio			
Video			
Web Site/E-mail			

C. Develop New Strategies and Vehicles

Communications Objective 1

Target Audience:

State Objective:

Which vehicles will you use, how will you use them, and why are they good strategic choices?

☐ **Face-to-Face:**

☐ **Print:**

☐ **Audio:**

☐ **Video:**

☐ **Web Site/E-mail:**

☐ **Other:**

Communications Objective 2

Target Audience:

State Objective:

Which vehicles will you use, how will you use them, and why are they good strategic choices?

☐ **Face-to-Face:**

☐ **Print:**

☐ **Audio:**

☐ **Video:**

☐ **Web Site/E-mail:**

☐ **Other:**

Communications Objective 3

Target Audience:

State Objective:

Which vehicles will you use, how will you use them, and why are they good strategic choices?

☐ **Face-to-Face:**

☐ **Print:**

☐ **Audio:**

☐ **Video:**

☐ **Web Site/E-mail:**

☐ **Other:**

Communications Objective 4

Target Audience:

State Objective:

Which vehicles will you use, how will you use them, and why are they good strategic choices?

☐ **Face-to-Face:**

☐ **Print:**

☐ **Audio:**

☐ **Video:**

☐ **Web Site/E-mail:**

☐ **Other:**

Communications Objective 5

Target Audience:

State Objective:

Which vehicles will you use, how will you use them, and why are they good strategic choices?

☐ **Face-to-Face:**

☐ **Print:**

☐ **Audio:**

☐ **Video:**

☐ **Web Site/E-mail:**

☐ **Other:**

Communications Objective 6

Target Audience:

State Objective:

Which vehicles will you use, how will you use them, and why are they good strategic choices?

☐ **Face-to-Face:**

☐ **Print:**

☐ **Audio:**

☐ **Video:**

☐ **Web Site/E-mail:**

☐ **Other:**

Step Six
Evaluate Your Efforts

A. Strategy for Evaluation

Define the purpose of the evaluation. What activities are you planning to evaluate? Will you be measuring communication activities or communication impact? Who is the target audience?

Who will be on the evaluation team?

List the measurable aspects of your communications objectives in the first column and indicate how you intend to measure those aspects in the second column.

B. Develop Outcome Measures

Reexamine the communications objectives you created. List 3 measurable activities and 3 measurable impacts below. If need be, revise the communications objective to be sure you are measuring both impact and activities.

Communications Objective 1

Activities to Measure:
1.
2.
3.

Impacts to Measure:
1.
2.
3.

State or revise the communications objective to demonstrate impact:

Communications Objective 2

Activities to Measure:
1.
2.
3.

Impacts to Measure:
1.
2.
3.

State or revise the communications objective to demonstrate impact:

Communications Objective 3

Activities to Measure:
1.
2.
3.

Impacts to Measure:
1.
2.
3.

State or revise the communications objective to demonstrate impact:

Communications Objective 4

Activities to Measure:
1.
2.
3.

Impacts to Measure:
1.
2.
3.

State or revise the communications objective to demonstrate impact:

Communications Objective 5

Activities to Measure:
1.
2.
3.

Impacts to Measure:
1.
2.
3.

State or revise the communications objective to demonstrate impact:

Communications Objective 6

Activities to Measure:
1.
2.
3.

Impacts to Measure:
1.
2.
3.

State or revise the communications objective to demonstrate impact:

Step Seven
Create a Timeline and Budget

A. Develop a Calendar

Write the month, date, activity, and person responsible for each task involved in implementing each strategy. Note events, holidays, lunch dates, etc.

Due date	Action/Task/Event/Holiday, Etc.	Person responsible

B. Communications Budget Sheet

Strategy/Tasks	Target date	Cost

APPENDIX 1

Planet 3000 Strategic Communications Worksheets

Worksheet 1 Mission Statement and Goals

Project Goals

Name of Organization: Planet 3000

Mission Statement
Planet 3000 is committed to healing the earth. Using research into natural ecosystems, Planet 3000 develops policy recommendations and pilot projects that apply these underlying principles to human ecosystems, such as cultural habits, social structures, commercial ventures, and the like.   It advocates for the establishment of human ecosystems that are in harmony with other life on the planet. By bringing the human social order into balance with ecological principles, diversity of all living things can be sustained and the evolutionary process that has guided and nurtured life on this planet can continue unabated.

Our 20- to 25-Word Organization Description
Planet 3000 advances scientifically backed research to preserve and protect natural ecosystems that benefit individuals and communities.

Goals
1. To pass a comprehensive transportation/clean air policy initiative to create a better quality of life through ecologically friendly transportation initiatives and stronger clean air standards.
2. To build a national network of businesses and environmentalists who will advance strong economic arguments and strategies to ensure that legislation is based on fiscally viable solutions.
3. To develop strategies to encourage individuals to personally commit to restoring a balance between themselves as individuals and the environment that we aspire to create and maintain.

Situation Analysis

A. Examining the External Environment

Demographic Forces: Has there been a shift or change in the populations or the makeup of the communities you serve? If yes, what does that mean? If no, is that cause for alarm?

While there are obvious demographic shifts happening in the country and the world as leadership is handed off to a younger generation of policy makers, there is also an opportunity to reach out to the children of baby boomers who helped launch the first Earth Day and were at the forefront of the environmental movement. It is our hope that they have passed on this enthusiasm for ecosystem protection to their children. It will be one of the research priorities during the first six months of this project.

Economic Forces: How do donors perceive our organization, and what does that mean for our financial future (consider government funding, foundations, and corporate contributors)? Is the economy shifting in ways that will cause a growth or a decline in demand for services from the populations we serve?

The recent partnership with the National Chambers of Commerce has given new vitality to our organization. Our major donors and chief foundation supporters see this partnership as giving us added credibility and potential for achieving some of our programmatic goals.

Furthermore, recent business alliances, such as the Business Environmental Leadership Council and other initiatives, have committed to a range of proactive measures to address climate change and the need for increased energy efficiency. We see many opportunities for new strategic partnerships in the immediate future.

People seem to be more concerned with quality-of-life issues, which has worked for our organization in the past. While we don't view our work as a quality-of-life concern, the fact is that the vast majority of people need to feel secure before they will venture off into an area that requires dramatic change. There are messaging opportunities around the need for change in order to ensure quality of life.

Technological Forces: What are the latest trends in business technology that we might use to become more cost effective? What are the latest products or trends in online technology that could impact our program areas of interest: program development, technical assistance, volunteer recruitment, training, education, and so on? How will these trends impact our organization? Can we afford to apply this technology to create a better product, provide improved services, and conduct more cost-effective advocacy efforts?

The staff has initiated a recommendation for videoconferencing and satellite hookups this year to experiment with linking the six target communities in an interactive way. A team of our researchers is working with several outside experts to develop a CD-ROM simulation that allows individuals to witness what happens when specific ecosystem principles are introduced into a variety of human systems. Ideally, we hope to be able to market this as a commercial education product.

Political Forces: What do we expect to be on the national, local, and state political agenda this year? Could it affect our organization or the populations we serve? If the winds blow our way, what can we expect? If they go against us, what is the worst that can happen? Is there something we are **not** seeing?

When the hole in the stratospheric ozone layer was detected, Republicans and Democrats, rich nations and poor nations, businesspeople and scientists all came together to shape a solution. There exists an opportunity to build new political alliances to advance this policy agenda. There are also forces out there that oppose this approach. We will need to be strategic about forging alliances and attentive to the fact that other policy priorities seem to have greater resonance with policy makers at this time.

Our strategy of building an unusual alliance of environmentalists and businesses with sound, economically based recommendations is the best way of approaching a broad spectrum of policy makers from both sides of the aisle. We hope that our pilot projects in six communities—with the communities themselves addressing policy makers—will attract political attention. The environmental coalition makes major efforts in each political cycle that should also support and inform our work with policy makers. Our town hall meetings can be valuable forums for elected officials.

Social Forces: What social or cultural trends are we seeing in the community, in the state, in the nation? What does this mean for our organization and its work? What social or cultural values do our constituents subscribe to? Have these values changed recently? If so, why? Does that impact our relationship to our constituents? What is the "mood" of the nation? Our community? What is the latest fear in society? What is the latest demand? What is the latest "hope" or "solution" being talked about? How could these fears, demands, and hopes impact our work?

Although the mood of the country is positive, there is a growing concern about the environment and an increase in individual actions for recycling and smart use. While people seem intrigued by natural laws, they also don't recognize their own connection to these laws.

While our staff prefers a positive approach to the issue, we realize that fear is a great motivator for driving the public agenda and getting the public's attention.

Episodic/personal frame: In a world spinning out of control, a more balanced life is possible. Learn how the laws of nature can improve your life.

Systemic/public policy frame: Natural ecosystems have nurtured life on the planet for millions of years. Yet we are destroying our planet, one law at a time. The wrong law at the wrong time. Turn it around. Research shows that we can change our policies and save our planet.

Current framing of our issue is not helpful. "Ecosystems are vulnerable" seems too vague for most citizens to embrace as an issue where they can make a difference OR that policy makers can address, at the national and global level. Many on staff fear that the politicians will never reach consensus about the right solutions.

B. Examining the Internal Environment

Management objectives: Are there clear management objectives in the Standard Operating Procedures of the organization (the SOP)? Is staff aware of the management objectives of the organization and what that means for their job performance? How do they relate to program objectives? Have we defined what each management objective means and why it is important for the organization's success? Is there input or feedback from the staff?

Planet 3000 is a very experimental and open institution. We are not afraid to take risks and to undertake confrontational or controversial tactics to draw attention to our work. We spend a lot of time talking about radical theories for safeguarding the ecosystem.

The recent completion of our strategic plan with three clear goals is a major step for Planet 3000. We now have greater clarity of what the priorities are and how we, as an organization, will measure our success. Furthermore, the new alliance with the National Chambers of Congress gives us a unique partner that enhances our credibility and gives us added resources for achieving our mission.

The challenge now is for middle management to come together around these goals and to create a communications strategic plan and a work plan to tap resources across the organization to achieve our goals. We need new ways of working together if we are going to be successful.

Financial Resources: Are our financial resources covering our existing activities? Do we pay our expenses in a timely manner? Do we have a reserve fund? Do we have a core group of supporters and donors? Does this base need to be expanded?

While Planet 3000 has sound business systems and financial management, we do not have a reserve fund. As an advocacy nonprofit, we believe that our donors expect us to use their contributions to make a difference not to save for a rainy day.

The new initiatives outlined in our current strategic plan have been well received by major foundations, and our development team has ideas about forging partnerships with major business and corporate partners. If this overall initiative is successful, we will be able to reposition ourselves in terms of our funding base and then to expand programs and services, beyond this legislative initiative.

We have met our budgets over the past three years and expect to do so this year as well.

Physical Infrastructure: Does the organization have enough workspace for staff, consultants, and temporary workers? Is the space conducive to teamwork? Are there adequate light, air, and heat? Can people have a private conversation if they need to? Is the neighborhood safe for staff working odd hours? Is there room to expand if we take on new programs?

Our office provides workspace and conference space for current staff. However, as this initiative takes off and we are working in 75 congressional districts, we will need stronger regional presence. Plans are currently under way with the National Chambers of Commerce to identify separate workspace for this campaign and to develop a regional structure, possibly housed in local or state Chamber offices.

We will also need to enhance our Web presence and to become more visible in cyberspace.

Technology Infrastructure: Do people have adequate computers and software to perform their jobs? Are there an adequate number of phone lines so that callers do not experience a busy signal? Are we maximizing the use of our printers? Our telephone system? Do we have access to a VCR and monitor? To a video camcorder? Does staff do a lot of conference calling? Is it worth buying a phone made especially for conference calls?

Present office equipment and supplies meet the needs of current personnel. We are going to need to greatly expand our infrastructure for this campaign: more conference calls, internet capability, online presence, etc. Fortunately, the National Chambers of Commerce have systems in place that can support this campaign, and we have business partners who are eager to help ensure that we aren't restricted by inadequate technology.

Timing and preparation are two key concerns.

Worksheet 2 Strengths, Weaknesses, Opportunities, Threats

What are our strengths?

Strong relationships with the National Chambers of Commerce.

Strong relationships with national environmental groups.

New relationships with potential business and corporate allies.

Strong strategic plans and a clear sense of what needs to happen. Staff committed to making sure that we succeed.

What are our weaknesses?

No direct ties with business media or local media in our targeted communities.

No strong national spokesperson.

Need to create a national infrastructure over the next 6 months.

What opportunities exist in the next 18 months?

We have been invited to be the keynote address and campaign focus of the National Chambers of Commerce Annual Meeting in Washington, DC, in July.

What threats exist in the next 18 months?

The National Association of Manufacturers and the National Institute of Small Businesses are both on record opposing single, comprehensive legalization on this issue.

Our goals for this campaign are very ambitious—we have the potential for getting pulled off message and off strategy.

Worksheet 3 Analyze Strengths, Weaknesses, Opportunities, Threats

	Opportunities	Threats
Strengths	National Chambers of Commerce Annual Meeting—keynote in May. Strong support from businesses in the Northeast and Midwest. Plan to conduct a national survey to assess public support; to be used with members of Congress and the business community. The six pilot cities have their own structures, credibility, and volunteer networks with media and political leaders; they are well positioned to make the plan work.	National Association of Manufacturers and the National Institute for Small Businesses are on record as opposing comprehensive legislation. We don't know what the political agendas are for other environmental colleagues: whether they will complement or compete with our plan. We are dependent on the six pilot cities—this effort is only as strong as they are.
Weaknesses	No national recognized/celebrity spokesperson. No direct relationships with national press or business press in the targeted congressional districts.	Potential to get pulled off message and off strategy by esoteric discussions around research OR by the global discussion around ecosystems and environmental protections. We must stay focused for this pilot project to succeed.

Unique opportunity for the next six months:

- Launch six-city pilot project
- Showcase grassroots campaign at national Chamber of Commerce annual meeting
- National survey of public opinion attitudes

Challenge to address in the next six months:

- Staying focused
- Staying on message
- Preventing visible dissent

Worksheet 4 Form a Communications Action Team (CAT)

1. What skills or expertise do we need on our communications action team?

   The CAT should include conference coordinators, media relations staff, and outreach coordinators with ties to the business community, public affairs staff, and someone from the development office.

2. What internal representation do we want from our organization?

   The public affairs, communications, development, and conference coordination team.

3. Should we include external stakeholders (who and how many)?

   Contacts from the National Chambers of Commerce and national environment groups.

Names of Individuals for Action Team	What They Bring to the Team
Sally	Communications Director, media strategist, and has ties to the National Chamber of Commerce press office; will act as spokesperson and project coordinator
Tamar	Media liaison, expert at building the message strategies that will intrigue the business press and engage them in the critical importance of passing this legislation
Buddy	Public Affairs Director, working with the advocacy team and congressional offices to track the legislation supporting the initiative; ties with other organizations that also care about this issue
Steve	Conference Coordinator for the National Chambers of Commerce, handling all program logistics for the press conference, keynote address, and spokesperson relations
John	Experience working with broad array of association and other community groups; keeping everyone informed and with the program
Sam	Contact with key donors and major foundations, can help identify additional resources for the survey, published materials, and conference expenses

Publics that May Be Connected to Your Organization

Category/Name	For/Against	Reason for Connection Competitive
Place a check in front of those organizations with which your organization might collaborate. **Colleagues at other organizations**		**Stake in Organization Status**
John Raym	F A	Executive Director of environmental coalition
Pamela Scholler	F A	Leading researcher of ecosystems
Michael Estes	F A	Program officer of our largest funder
Organizations with similar program interests and values		
Environmental Working Group	F A	environmental policy research + education
Centrist	F A	conservation + new econometric. models + ecosystems
The National Audubon Society	F A	conserve/restore ecosystems, well-being of human civilization
Natural Resources Defense Council	F A	"stewardship of the earth"
The Nature Conservancy	F A	protection of ecosystems/resource management
Organizations that oppose our work		
Lambda Alpha International	F A	Land economics researchers
American Land Rights Association	F A	Wise use—people first and only
National Center for Public Policy Research	F A	Wise use research group
Center for Defense of	F A	Wise use advocacy and education
Free Enterprise Activists/Advocates	F A	Care about environment/understand the importance of ecosystems and believe human systems can change
Board members	F A	Committed to organization's mission 100%
Private foundations		
Pew Charitable Trusts	F A	Care about ecosystems; needs to see connection to human systems development
W. Alton Jones Foundation	F A	Understands connection of ecosystems to human systems
Joyce Mertz-Gilmore Foundation	F A	Care about ecosystems; needs to see connection to human systems development

Turner Foundation	F A	Understands connection of eco. systems to human systems
Corporate foundations		
AMR/American	F A	Environmental support (board connection)
Gannett	F A	Supports public education on environment
Donors	F A	75% have at least 3-year history
Community leaders	F A	Majority view ecosystems as irrelevant to their communities
Community groups/Local environmental groups (target 6 communities in 6 regions; partners for town meetings)		
Madison in the Balance	F A	Studies ecosystems in Midwest
Life and Harmony in Phoenix	F A	More focused on pollution/ population needs to see connection to ecosystems
Baltimore Eco-more	F A	Studies ecosystems in Maryland/ Delaware/District of Columbia
Boston in Balance	F A	Research and advocacy for New England ecosystems (partners with Kennedy School of Government, Harvard University)
South Florida Lives	F A	New group; focused on restoring ecosystems
Iowans for the Earth	F A	Working to reestablish prairies
Organized religious groups	F A	Against evolutionary theory; humans do God's work
Reporters, editors		
Tom Abrams, *NY Times*	F A	Scientist; understands ecosystems; challenges connection to possible human systems
Regina Elderson, *Wash. Post*	F A	Political reporter; likes the concept
Ronnie Langley, *Newsweek*	F A	Good on environmental issues; has not been linked to our assertion that there is a need for human systems change
Jonathan Orris, *US News & World Report*	F A	Subscribes to free market approach
Government officials/policy makers		
Ellis McGill, Environmental Protection Agency Chief	F A	Sees us as one of many voices in the mix
Joanna Shatzkin, Secretary of Interior	F A	Need to get ecosystems on radar screen

Sarah Jonis, Chief, National Economic Council	F A	Seems interested in theory; not sure about accepting practical implication tests
Parents	F A	Strongly represented of donor/activist base
Educators/Teachers	F A	Use organization's curriculum materials
Business: corporations, associations, leaders		
Able Technology	F A	Researching ecosystem laws for ideas for new products and processes
Wainwright Industries	F A	Southwest mining; support wise use
National Chambers of Commerce	F A	Interested in pilot test w/select members
Children and youth	F A	Planet 3000's next generation program
Healthcare providers	F A	Healthy Planet, Healthy Lives program
Others		
Researchers and academics (allied theories)	F A	Use their work; need participation/leadership
Researchers and academics (wise use theories)	F A	They pose strong argument to issue
Researchers and academics (neutral/undecided)	F A	They're critical in validating theory

Worksheet 5 Community Partners and Stakeholders

List all of the organizations, groups, and individuals in each category that are critical to your organization. Consider why they are important to your organization. Place a check in front of those organizations with which your organization might collaborate.

Category/Name	Reason for Connection

Colleagues at other organizations

_____   _____
_____   _____
_____   _____
_____   _____
_____   _____
_____   _____
_____   _____

Organizations with similar program interests and values or with whom we partner

_____   _____
_____   _____
_____   _____
_____   _____
_____   _____
_____   _____
_____   _____

Organizations that oppose our work

_____   _____
_____   _____
_____   _____
_____   _____
_____   _____
_____   _____
_____   _____

Clients_____

Activists/advocates (for us)_____

Activists/advocates (against us)_____

Board members_____

Volunteers_____

Category/Name	Reason for Connection
Private foundations	
_____	_____
_____	_____
_____	_____
_____	_____
Corporate foundations	
_____	_____
_____	_____
_____	_____
_____	_____
Donors	
_____	_____
_____	_____
_____	_____
_____	_____
Community leaders	
_____	_____
_____	_____
_____	_____
_____	_____
_____	_____
_____	_____
Community groups	
_____	_____
_____	_____
_____	_____
_____	_____
_____	_____
Church groups	
_____	_____
_____	_____
_____	_____
_____	_____
_____	_____

Category/Name	Reason for Connection

Reporters, editors, media outlets, specific programs

Government officials/policy makers

Non-government policy makers

Parents

Educators/teachers

Corporations—senior managers

Small business owners

Category/Name	Reason for Connection
Youth	
_____	_____
_____	_____
_____	_____
_____	_____
Healthcare providers	
_____	_____
_____	_____
_____	_____
_____	_____
_____	_____
Social service agencies	
_____	_____
_____	_____
_____	_____
_____	_____
_____	_____
_____	_____
_____	_____
_____	_____
_____	_____
_____	_____

Review your list and select at least 5 priority audiences that will be the focal point of your strategic communication efforts.

1. _____
2. _____
3. _____
4. _____
5. _____

Worksheet 6 Audience Identification

Step 1. Review the list below and rate each "audience" in terms of its importance to your work (somewhat important, critically important or not applicable).

Step 2. Decide whether you have been effective or not effective at reaching out to each audience.

Step 3. Rank the 5 most critical audiences for this planning process. Check the appropriate boxes.

Category	Step 1 N/A	Step 1 Somewhat Important	Step 1 Critical	Step 2 Not Effective	Step 2 Effective	Step 3 Rank the Top 5
National Chamber of Commerce			X	1 2 3	X 5	4
National Environmental Groups		X		1 2 3	X 5	5
Nationally active—environmental ativists		X		1 2 3	X 5	
Local Chambers of Commerce			X	1 2 X	4 5	1
Local environmental groups			X	1 2 X	4 5	2
Locally active—environmental activists			X	1 2 X	4 5	3
Business press				1 2 3	X 5	
Local media in targeted markets				1 2 X	4 5	
John Raym—Executive Director of environmental coalition				1 2 3	4 X	

Pamela Scholler—leading researcher on ecosystems				1 2 3	4 X	
Environmental working groups				1 2 3	4 X	
The Nature Conservancy				1 2 3	4 X	
American Land Rights Association—opposition				1 X 3	4 5	
Pew Charitable Trusts—funds similar work				1 2 3	4 X	
Turner Foundation—funds similar work				1 2 3	X 5	
Researchers and academicians				1 2 X	4 5	
High school teachers—civics classes				1 2 X	4 5	
Essential to pick the right pilot sites						

Worksheet 7 (A) Audience Profile

Audience: Fairfax County VA Chamber of Commerce

1. Describe your audience: What are their concerns? What characteristics of your audience are important to your organization (e.g., their education levels, income levels, family size, health issues)?

   Made up of local business and commercial leaders, the Fairfax County Chamber's mission is to develop, encourage, and promote the economic vitality, quality of life, and political interests of its members and the business of northern Virginia for the benefit of the broader community. It has a mailing list of approximately 5,000 individuals engaged in business within the county. This chapter of the Chamber has one primary concern: the transportation crisis and finding new funding strategies to address road improvements.

2. Why are they important to you?

   Fairfax County will be one of the six pilot sites for this campaign. It is adjacent to the nation's capital and has strong working relationships with adjacent counties. Its legislative priorities make it a natural match for this campaign.

3. Why should your audience care about your organization and its issues?

   This campaign will be highlighted at the annual meeting and gives the Fairfax Chapter an opportunity to be showcased at the national convention. This campaign will give them added resources and additional messages to use with policy makers about the need to have ecosystem approaches to solving local transportation needs.

4. What do you want from this audience?

   To be active participants in the 6-month campaign, to recruit supporters from their members, vendors, and other community partnerships; to engage in the forum and other events leading up to the national meeting; to participate in "Lobby Day" and meet with their elected representatives and actively represent this campaign at the annual meeting.

5. How does this audience receive information?

   At monthly Chamber events, through the newsletter and from the Chamber Web site.

6. Are there particular individuals who have credibility or power over the target audience? What are their names?

   The members of the board and other leadership positions.

7. Are there other individuals who can help you better reach this target audience? Who?

   The mayor and other county leaders from the board of supervisors.

8. How will you know if you have successfully reached this audience?

   By their active participation in the campaign and the amount of support they generate through the petition drive.

Worksheet 7(B) Audience Profile

Audience: National Audubon Society

1. Describe your audience: What are their concerns? What characteristics of your audience are important to your organization (e.g., their education levels, income levels; family size, health issues)?

   The National Audubon Society's mission is to conserve and restore natural ecosystems, focusing on birds, other wildlife, and their habitats for the benefit of humanity and the earth's biological diversity. The society has a national network of community-based nature centers and chapters that offer scientific and educational programs and encourage millions of people to advocate for sound policies annually.

2. Why are they important to you?

   In the six pilot cities, we hope to host some of our educational and recruitment programs at their nature centers. The staff and volunteers are logical partners for our campaign and can provide important subject expertise and community support for the campaign. Many of our Chamber members are also active in their local nature centers.

3. Why should your audience care about your organization and its issues?

   We have overlapping missions and share the same commitment to sound policy to preserve natural ecosystems. They are a national partner in support of this legislative initiative.

4. What do you want from this audience?

   To provide scientific expertise, to encourage their member nature centers to participate in local activities, and to be an active participant in the national campaign.

5. How does this audience receive information?

   Regular newsletters, Web site, and updates from the national office to the nature centers. Large and supportive national staff that are routinely in touch with the field.

6. Are there particular individuals who have credibility or power over the target audience? What are their names?

   The public affairs staff and the regional staff ae enthusiastic and they will be essential to our success as well as the heads of the nature centers in each of the pilot cities.

7. Are there other individuals that can help you better reach this target audience? Who?

   Some of the local Chamber leaders will also be helpful with this.

8. How will you know if you have successfully reached this audience?

   By their active participation in the campaign and the amount of support they generate through the petition drive.

Worksheet 8 Develop SMART Communications Objectives

Remember that communications objectives focus on the cycle of the communications process (to inform, engage, motivate to act, and maintain relationships). Communications objectives have action verbs (e.g., educate, teach, inform, provide, conduct, enlist, mobilize, discuss, promote, build consensus).

Communications Objective 1

Target Audience: Small business owners

> Number: 75
> Congressional
> Districts

Select One: ☐ Inform   ☐ Engage   XX Motivate   ☐ Maintain

Desired Action: To contact their members of Congress to support the legislation for better transportation and clean air policies.

Target Date: April–September

State Objective: Small business owners in each congressional district will have met with their member of Congress and encouraged them to support the initiative on better transportation and clear air policies.

Communications Objective 2

Target Audience: Members of Congress

> Number: 75

Select One: ☐ Inform   ☐ Engage   XX Motivate   ☐ Maintain

Desired Action: By September 30, 75 members of Congress from the Northeast and Midwest will vote to pass the initiative on better transportation and clean air policies.

Target Date: September 30

State Objective: By the end of the fiscal year, 75 members of Congress will have heard from their constituents about the importance of this legislation and will have voted to pass the initiative.

Worksheet 9 Language Worksheet

Words I Currently Use to Describe My Organization or the Work We Do:
Episodic/personal frame: In a world spinning out of control, a more balanced life is possible. Learn how the laws of nature can change your life.

Words to Avoid When Talking about My Organization and the Work that It Does:
Ecosystem is a hard word for nonenvironmentalists to get their arms around. We need to talk about impact that is closer to the communities where people live.   When talking with environmentalists, we tend to talk about saving the earth for future generations. For this campaign, we need to be sensitive about providing hard data about the economic impacts for the small businesses that are our new partners.

New Words that Could Have the Greatest Impact on My Target Audience:
Systemic/public policy frame: Natural ecosystems have nurtured life on the planet for millions of years. Yet we are destroying our planet, one law at a time, the wrong laws at the wrong time. Turn it around. The right law at the right time.

Tips: Test each word: Does it convey an emotion? Does it have impact? Does it have meaning to civilians? Is it persuasive?

Worksheet 10 Organization Description

Our Current Organization Description
Planet 3000 is a nonprofit research and advocacy organization committed to increasing public awareness of the natural ecosystems that have nurtured life on the planet for millions of years. We seek to help individuals incorporate the laws of nature into their daily living to enhance their lives and improve our communities. (51 words)

What is the impression we want to make?

We want individuals and policy makers to adopt personal practices and enact legislation to preserve and protect natural ecosystems.

What two facts do we want everyone to know about us?

1. Our policy recommendations are based on scientific research.
2. We partner with policy makers, environmental groups, and small businesses to advance policies that have demonstrable economic impact and will improve our communities.

Our 20- to 25-Word Organization Description
Planet 3000 advances scientifically backed research to preserve and protect natural ecosystems that benefit individuals and communities.

Worksheet 11(A) Develop Persuasive Messages

Create a message for each of your priority audiences. It should have three parts: Identify the issue and desired change, make it relevant to the audience, and provide an action step that they can take. Write your message as a complete sentence or two. Try to use the most persuasive language, and use the word *you* at least once.

Target Audience: Visitors to the local nature centers

Desired Change: Attend a public forum to learn more

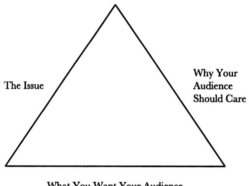

The Issue

Why Your
Audience
Should Care

What You Want Your Audience
To Do, Think, or Feel

Part 1 (Issue) We are working with national environmental groups and local businesses to advance legislation to improve our local communities.

Part 2 (Why Your Audience Should Care) As someone who obviously cares about nature, we think you would be a great partner in helping our campaign send a strong message to Congress.

Part 3 (What You Want Your Audience to Do, Think, or Feel) Please join us at a town hall meeting on October 1 to learn more.

Now write a message combining all 3 parts **as if you are talking to the audience.**

In a world spinning out of control, a more balanced life is possible. Natural ecosystems have nurtured life on the planet for millions of years. We are launching a campaign to improve our communities. Join Planet 3000 at Town Hall on October 1 to learn how the laws of nature can enhance your life and your community.

Worksheet 11(B) Develop Persuasive Messages

Create a message for each of your priority audiences. It should have three parts: Identify the issue and desired change, make it relevant to the audience, and provide an action step that they can take. Write your message as a complete sentence or two. Try to use the most persuasive language, and use the word *you* at least once.

Target Audience: Small business leaders

Desired Change: Attend the forum

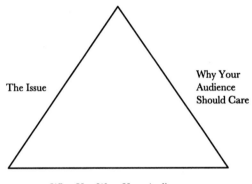

The Issue

Why Your
Audience
Should Care

What You Want Your Audience
To Do, Think, or Feel

Part 1 (Issue) We are partnering with the National Chambers of Commerce to advance legislation to improve our communities with research-based policies that have a proven impact on local economies.

Part 2 (Why Your Audience Should Care) As a business leader who cares about the community and your neighbors, we invite you to join with other members of the local Chamber of Commerce to learn more about the campaign and how you can help.

Part 3 (What You Want Your Audience to Do, Think, or Feel) Please join us at a town hall meeting on October 1 to learn more.

Now write a message combining all 3 parts **as if you are talking to the audience.**

This legislative campaign, sponsored with the National Chamber of Commerce, is designed to improve our communities and our neighborhoods through research based practices with proven economic benefits. Join us at a town hall meeting on October 1 to learn more.

Worksheet 12 Put a Human Face on Your Work

One anecdote about our work that puts a "human face" on our project is:

> Working with the local Chambers of Commerce, we want to host forums at their monthly meetings where community leaders and their guests can hear the results of our public opinion survey and an overview of the proposed legislation and participate in a discussion about the difference this legislation can make in their community.
>
> Working with our national business media contacts, we will highlight the support of the local Chambers for this initiative.

A second anecdote about our work that puts a human face on our project is:

> Working with the local nature centers, we hope to engage young people and their parents in discussions about how they can make decisions at home that will help preserve natural ecosystems and make their community a healthier place to live.

Vehicles and Strategies for Planet 3000

Planet 3000 is planning to mobilize small business owners from 75 congressional districts in 6 pilot cities to support a comprehensive transportation/clean air policy initiative. Some strategies developed by the staff for consideration include:

1. Conducting a poll to assess depth of support for this policy among the targeted audience group and alternative community actions for ensuring passage of the legislation. The findings would be released at a press conference held in conjunction with the National Chambers of Commerce Annual Meeting. Potential for making the legislation a national policy priority for the Chambers and expand the pilot project for Year 2.
2. Distribute radio actualities and video news releases (VNRs) highlighting the poll findings to focus attention on the impact of traffic on air quality and the air quality standards in the proposed legislation and to solicit community participation through local Chambers.

3. Host town hall meetings in advance of the annual meeting, circulating petitions and gathering support for the legislation. Business accounts of how they are changing the way that they do business will provide more incentives for legislators to support "proven practices."
4. Recruit a "celebrity" spokesperson to present at the National Chambers of Commerce Annual Meeting in Washington, DC. Do a satellite media tour and a "Lobby Day" on Capitol Hill, with media escorting the celebrity spokesperson to select member offices.
5. Create a home page for the business-for-business campaign with links to local groups in the 75 targeted congressional districts. Encourage peer-to-peer sharing of strategies and successes in engaging community business partners and meeting with local officials. Templates for the town meetings and other tools could also be posted for the pilot projects.

Expected Audience Response

The first strategy will not only help staff assess the target audience's opinions more accurately but provides additional grassroots credibility for our work with the Chamber and policy makers. Local reporters and media outlets in the targeted districts will also have the data to supplement the human face that we will put on the story through the town hall meetings.

Planet 3000 staff also expect the target audience will be responsive because of the link to the national Chambers' interest and the endorsement of their local chapters. The celebrity spokesperson will also add credibility with the target audience and cache for this initiative.

The Web strategy also provides friendly peer-to-peer competition across the pilot projects and can demonstrate local successes, making it harder for those involved to say "This can't be done." The combination of all this local effort and activity will help demonstrate to policy makers and others the growing strength of the movement and the support behind the passing of the proposed legislation.

Organization's Relationship to the Audience

Planet 3000 does not have any current relationship with the local small business communities that have been targeted. It is relying on its relationship with the national Chambers and its outreach partnerships to make this initiative happen. While these relationships appear strong, there is a lot riding on the targeting of the right pilot cities and the right community partners. There will be pressure on the Planet 3000 staff to make sure that the project is well managed and pleasurable for all the partners involved.

Planet 3000 will continue to work with the National Chamber of Commerce and cultivate members of the business press. By conducting the poll and the local impact information, Planet 3000 serves the business community while advancing its mission and policy agenda.

Strategy Influences Perception

The National Chamber of Commerce endorsement of this effort and the use of business-focused arguments and rationales create a natural synergy that should excite local businesses. The challenge for Planet 3000 will be to ensure continued momentum and the sense that this partnership is local and beneficial to both. We will want to minimize too much emphasis on the research part of our organization and highlight the advocacy and activism of the grassroots business partners.

The approach is based on a strongly rational model, framed in economic and business terms about the bottom line. Planet 3000 will highlight the links between the policy guidelines and its support of local business interests. By relying on the business press, the Chambers of Commerce, and local reporters to deliver the message, Planet 3000 hopes to reach other businesses, their vendor partners, and their customers, greatly expanding the base of support for the legislation and the outreach to policy makers.

Control of the Message

Planet 3000 will have some control over the message through the survey data and the Web site, but the organization has made a calculated decision to rely on local business leaders, the Chambers, and other business interests to be the major spokespeople in this initiative. The organization will have to ensure that all spokespeople stay on message, reinforcing key points as well as the desired frame that will effectively position the issue and the stories in the media. Even the radio actualities and the VNR will be important pieces of the strategy for "staying on message."

The fact that the target audience will be more receptive to messages delivered by these spokespeople outweighs the limited control that Planet 3000 will have over how the message unfolds during the campaign. The engagement materials and the Web site, while reaching the primary audience in its original form, will also be used and modified by the local groups in ways that will go beyond the organization's control.

Effort to Implement

Planet 3000 has spent the past 6 months building the bridges that are necessary to make these strategies happen. It also has a 5-person communications and public affairs team that will manage and implement the strategies. A working team with 3 representatives from each of the pilot sites has also been meeting regularly by conference call for the past 3 months and will start meeting weekly once the campaign is launched. There will be an outside consultant working full time to manage the growth of the Web site and to monitor the Web interaction during the campaign.

Budget Considerations

The strategies proposed are both high profile and expensive, but the organization sees this initiative as crucial to building its credibility and its base of support at the business, community, and national policy level. The board and senior leadership are committed to the campaign and have worked with funders and individual donors to build support for this initiative. The staff expects to keep the costs of the VNR to a minimum by using existing footage from its library and from local sources. It has negotiated a discounted package with the satellite feed company that will transmit the actuality and the VNR. Relying on Web transmissions of materials means that the local businesses and local Chambers will absorb many of the production costs for materials. The poll is also an expensive item, but it is serving a dual function regarded as essential to the campaign: shaping the actual messages and strategies and generating credibility with the press, the National Chamber of Commerce, and elected officials.

Potential Impact on Other Audiences

These strategies are designed to reinforce the campaign's key messages, to reach multiple audiences and, hopefully, to create a ripple effect: Business press, business-to-business outreach, vendor and customer outreach, targeted petitions, letters, and messages to Congress are designed to support the mission and advance the public policy agenda of Planet 3000. When all of these pieces work in concert with each other, we anticipate that this campaign will increase the grassroots base of the organization as much as tenfold.

Worksheet 13 Evaluating Strategic Options

Targeted Audience: Small Business Owners

Step 1. Review the strategic options under consideration and assign a numeric value (from 1 to 5, with 5 being the highest) for the effectiveness of each strategy against the seven criteria.

1. Responsive to audience: 1 unresponsive, 5 highly responsive
2. Appropriate relationship: 1 inappropriate, 5 builds on our strengths
3. Strategy affects perception: 1 emotional, 5 rational
4. Strategy affects message: 1 no control over message, 5 we control message
5. Effort to implement: 1 draws on our strengths, 5 will tax our capacity
6. Cost to implement: 1 least expensive, 5 most expensive
7. Impact on others: 1 no impact on others, 5 allows us to reach other targeted audiences

Step 2. Decide which strategies are the most likely to give you the desired result with the target audience.

Step 3. Rank order the effective strategies for this target audience and this strategic communications objective.

Strategy	Responsive to audience	Appropriate to relationship	Strategy affects perception	Strategy affects message	Effort to implement	Cost to implement	Impact on other audiences	Total	Rank order
Public opinion research	3	5	5	5	2	5	4	29	2
Radio actualities and VNRs	4	3	2	4	2	3	4	22	4
Town hall meetings	5	3	4	2	3 depends on business partners	4	5	26	1
Celebrity spokesperson	3	3	1	2-4 depends on person selected	2	4	4	19	5
Web site	4	3 new staff hire	3	5	2 easy with new hire	4	4	25	3

All of these strategies are designed to work in concert with each other and are mutually reinforcing.

Worksheet 14 Evaluate Existing Vehicles and Strategies

Step 1. List existing vehicles used by your organization.
Step 2. Identify priority audiences that could benefit from these vehicles.
Step 3. Verify that each vehicle carries the right message.
Step 4. Verify that the vehicle is effectively reaching the audience.

Step 1	Step 2	Step 3	Step 4
Vehicles we use	Primary audience	Conveys our message?	Effective at reaching the audience?
Face-to-Face			
1. Nature center presentations	Children and their parents	Yes	Yes
2. Town hall meetings	Community activists	Yes	Yes
3. Chamber meetings	Small business leaders	Yes	Yes
Print			
1. Public opinion survey	Policy makers/media	Yes	Yes
2. Campaign materials	Small business leaders	Yes	??
3.			
Audio			
1. Radio talk shows	All audiences	Yes	??
2. Press releases and media outreach	Media	Yes	??
3.			

Video			
1. Video news release	News media	Yes	??
2.			
3.			
Web site/E-mail			
1. New design for business campaign	Small business	Yes	??
2.			
3.			

Worksheet 15 Plan New Vehicles and Strategies

Communications Objective 1

Target Audience: Small business leaders in 6 pilot cities

State objective: Engage small business leaders and Chamber groups in the six pilot cities to lead the advocacy campaign, recruit petition signers, and present at the national conference

Which vehicles will you use, how will you use them, and why are they good strategic choices?

☐ **Face-to-Face** Presentation at National Chamber Meeting

Local town hall meetings: Get people to sign the petition

Nature centers: Get people to sign the petition

☐ **Print** Press releases: Number of stories run

Organizing kits: Number of events held

☐ **Audio** _____

_____

_____

☐ **Video** **VNR:** Number of placements, call-ins to the campaign

☐ **Web site/** Listserv and materials for the campaign:
E-Mail Number of visits to the site, interaction with field staff and other organizers

_____

☐ **Other** _____

_____

_____

Worksheet 16 Develop Outcome Measures

Reexamine the communications objectives you created for Worksheet 7. List three measurable activities *and* three measurable impacts below. If necessary, revise the communications objective to be sure you are measuring both impact and activities.

Communications Objective 1

Activities to Measure: Engage Chambers in 6 pilot cities:

1. Number of town hall meetings held; number of participants
2. Number of Chamber meetings held; number of small businesses recruited
3. Number of nature center programs held; number of parents and kids attending

Impacts to Measure:

1. Town hall meetings—number of signatures generated
2. Chamber meetings—number of businesses that will support campaign
3. Nature center programs—number of families that pledge to change practices

State or revise the communications objective to demonstrate impact:

Chamber groups in six cities will engage small businesses, community activists, and parents and families to support community change in a measurable way.

Communications Objective 2

Activities to Measure: Motivate 75 members of Congress from the Northeast and Midwest to vote for passage of the initiative on better transportation and clean air policies.

1. Number of meetings held in each congressional office with (a) small business leaders; (b) community activists; and (c) parents and families engaged in community change activities
2. Number of letters and petitions sent to each Member of Congress
3. Number of Members of Congress who sing as sponsors of the transportation initiative

Impacts to Measure:

1. Number of co-sponsors on the initiative from the 75 targeted states
2. Passage of the bill in sub-committee of the Appropriations Committee
3. Passage of the bill in committee of the Appropriations Committee
4. Passage of the bill by the House of Representatives and forwarded to the Senate for consideration

State or revise the communications objective to demonstrate impact:

75 Members of Congress from the Northeast and the Midwest will sponsor and support passage of the initiative on better transportation and clean air policies.

2

Essential Communications Tools

A nonprofit organization needs to educate or inform its constituencies and the public regarding its goal, objectives, and role in the community. Communications efforts are designed to promote the organization and to garner favorable opinions about its work, service, and community relationships. Communications should also project confidence in the organization and convey that it is a good place for staff and volunteers to work.[1]

A comprehensive communications plan includes supporting products that convey the core messages and image of the nonprofit:

Organization Description

- This is a 20- to 25-word description of the organization that describes it and *who* it serves. Often the organization description is called the "elevator speech" or the "cocktail party description" of the nonprofit. It should be in simple language. Many organizations miss this first opportunity to make a strong impression because they fail to describe who they are and what they do in a consistent manner. Some nonprofits describe themselves through their mission statements. In others, people associated with the organization create their own description, something that reflects their role in the nonprofit but not the entire work of the organization. When this happens, this description may change each time they are asked "Whom do you work for?" and "What do you do?" Clearly, both of these methods miss a valuable opportunity to create enthusiasm and excitement about the work that you do. Failing to tell the organization's story in a consistent and compelling way can cause confusion. For this reason, it is important to develop a brief description of your organization that all staff members, board members, and volunteers (indeed, all stakeholders)

---

[1]Barry J. McLeish, *Successful Marketing Strategies for Nonprofit Organizations* (New York: John Wiley & Sons, 1995).

should use all the time, uniformly. This step is an important one in building a stronger identity for your organization.

One-Page Fact Sheet

This document is the definitive description of the organization and what it does. The one-page fact sheet has four key elements:

1. Organization description
2. Brief historical statement about the organization
3. Summary of the programs and services offered by the organization
4. Contact information for reaching the organization

The purpose of the one-page fact sheet is to answer the question: What can our organization do for you?

Standard Press Kits

A press kit is built around a standard set of materials that can be used repeatedly whenever you host a press event. Among the items that should always be included in a press kit are:

- One-page fact sheet that includes the mission statement, organization description, and the services that the organization provides
- One-page profile of the spokespeople, including basic biographical information; offer to provide photographs upon request
- Issue briefs
- Contact list
- Press clippings

Optional items include:

- Annual report
- Copy of the latest newsletter
- List of coalition partners, sponsoring organizations or other relationships that represent how the organization does its work in the community

Annual Report

Many nonprofit organizations spend the majority of their communications budget on the development of their annual reports. Annual reports are an opportunity to present the essential financial information, including audit results. Annual reports are also an opportunity to document significant accomplishments and new programs and to highlight significant individuals who support the organization and benefit from its services. Annual reports are an important tool to demonstrate to community partners, key donors, and grant officers, where the money went and what it accomplished.

Brochures, Fact Cards, Question-and-Answer Sheets

Brochures, fact cards, and question-and-answer sheets are additional ways to get out the basic information about your organization and the work that it does. Desktop publishing software makes it easy to design nice-looking materials that can be narrowcast to reach specific targeted audiences.

IRS Form 990 Return of Organization Exempt from Income Tax

The 990 is the form that the IRS requires nonprofit organizations to submit. This public document includes (among other things) details of revenue and expenses for the year; details of expenses by program services, management, and fundraising; a description of activities related to the organization's exempt purpose; a statement of financial position; and a list of officers, directors, and trustees, including compensation paid to them. Schedule A of Form 990 requests a listing of the five highest-paid employees other than officers and directors, the five highest-paid persons for professional services, and details of revenues and expenses.

Portions of the 990 provide opportunities for informing the reader in greater detail about the organization. The Statement of Functional Expenses allows the organization to demonstrate low overhead, high expenditures on program activities and other examples of its financial management. The Statement on Program Service Accomplishments can be expanded to focus on the types of programs undertaken, the number of clients served, and the impact within the community. For more examples on how to use the 990 to promote the organization, see *The Nonprofit Legal Landscape* by Tom Hyatt (Board Source, 2005).[2]

Web Sites

Promoting an organization online is more than just establishing a Web site; it involves finding and posting relevant information, identifying and

---

[2]Ober Kaler, Attorneys At Law. *The Nonprofit Legal Landscape* (Washington, D.C.: Board Source, 2005).

connecting with current and potential audiences, and, possibly, developing your own online community. In other words, it is proactive, interactive, and ongoing.[3] A well-organized, well-written, well-maintained, and graphically compelling Web site is one of the best ways to educate and influence key constituencies.

The most effective Web sites are light, layered, and linked. That is:

- *Light.* The site is inviting and warm and encourages people to explore. There is enough information on the home page to show that viewers have come to the right location, but not so much that they feel bogged down by the information.
- *Layered.* The site has an index that invites users to delve deeper. It provides easy links back to the home page and cross-references the material within the site.
- *Linked.* Increasingly it is important for viewers to connect with other Web sites that provide related information, auxiliary services, and additional information or to review additional perspectives.

Web sites tend to develop in three phases:

1. Information provision
2. Information provision with limited membership feedback (sign-up, order materials, etc.
3. Fully integrated site that allows the visitor to interact with the host site

Step 3, if fully supported, can be a vehicle for fulfilling the nonprofit's mission.

Seal of Approval

The nonprofit might also seek to expand its identity by creating a seal of approval around products or issues that support or advance its mission. Other possible "seals of approval" might be certificates awarded to those who contribute to advancing the organization's mission, leadership awards for successful community actions, celebrity endorsers or spokespeople who lend their credibility to the organization, and programs that recognize volunteer leadership and student activists.

---

[3]Getting Started: Outreach via the Internet for Not-for-Profit or Public Sector Organizations, www.coyotecom.com/promote.html.

Elements of a Style Manual

A style manual is a form of rulebook that outlines the organization's approach to its brand and image. It helps the organization deliver its messages in a strong and consistent manner by setting the parameters for how each communication vehicle should look and feel. The style manual is a tool for ensuring that the message is delivered consistently throughout all elements of the organization's communications.

Every nonprofit should create and follow a style manual that includes the guidelines for use of the following design and language elements:

1. *Logo.* The first part of the style manual should address the logo—what it is designed to convey, the color process used for its creation, and the authorized color palette. It should also specify the guidelines for developing the logo in a black-and-white format.

2. *Logo variations.* This part should address the approved variations for the use of the logo. For example
   - Where and how the logo appears on a piece that is co-branded with another organization
   - When the logo appears on a colored background and will appear in relief
   - If the logo is being used with a subbrand of a program, campaign, or special project

   This section should demonstrate examples of logo use that are not appropriate, such as making the logo too small, crowding it with text or other colors, or placing it at an odd angle on the page.

3. *Fonts.* The style manual should specify the preferred fonts for all type used by the organization, including sans serif typeface for headlines.

4. *Formats.* The style manual can outline preferred designs for letterhead, mailing labels, business cards, and books, reports or other major publications for the organization.

5. *Language.* The style manual should provide guidelines for the use of language to describe the organization. At a minimum, the manual should provide the mission, value statement, organization description, tagline, or slogan and any other preferred words for describing the organization's programs and services. It should also identify those words that should *not* be used to describe the organization and its work.

6. *Photographs, graphics and other images.* The style manual can outline the preferred use of photographs and images in newsletters. This is to set guidelines to insure that the photos are large enough to be seen, that they focus on an activity that has been cropped to show it at best advantage, and to ensure that the pages are not too busy or the photographs and images distracting.

7. *Web guidelines.* Increasingly, style manuals also address the same design issues for the home page and other elements of Web sites. Common concerns include:
   • Where contact information is located
   • Where the logo is placed
   • The preferred font
   • Style recommendations for keeping language short and simple

4

Expanding the Organization's Coalitions and Partnerships

Nonprofit organizations are increasingly relying on coalitions and partnerships to fulfill their missions and outreach efforts in the community. An organization may decide that it needs to mobilize allies to help it achieve its strategic communications goals. These allies may include employees, clients/constituents, retirees, donors, and other stakeholders. They may also include organizations that are committed to the same goals and objectives, such as associations, business-oriented groups, policy leaders, public interest groups, community supporters, and the media. Many funding partners, policy makers, and community leaders look to nonprofit organizations to work in partnership in order to maximize community resources and to prevent duplication of effort.

Generally, these partnerships serve two broad purposes:

1. They generate visible public attention or support for the organization's mission and issues beyond its traditional sphere of influence.
2. They demonstrate and communicate the breadth and depth of this support to community leaders, policy makers, and other stakeholders.

Understanding Partnerships and Coalitions

Partnerships, coalitions, and working groups can help an organization strengthen the way it is perceived by the public and to extend its reach to new audiences. Community and coalition partners can help an organization test its messages and strategies to ensure their relevance in the community. Partners can help by reaching out to their base and to other allies where they have unique credibility, such as with religious or ethnic groups.

Advantages to Working in a Coalition

- *Win what couldn't be won alone.* Many issues require large numbers of people and many resources to win. Coalitions can pool people and resources to win important victories.
- *Build an ongoing power base and help increase the impact of individual organizations and their efforts.* Working in tandem expands the human and financial resources for major undertakings too vast for a single organization.
- *Develop new leaders.* Experienced leaders can be asked to take on coalition leadership roles, thus opening up slots to develop new leaders at the community or organization level.
- *Increase resources.* If the coalition's issue is central to the organization, the organization may directly benefit from coalition contributions of additional staff dedicated to the project, and donations of volunteer time and money.
- *Broaden scope.* A coalition may provide the opportunity for the non-profit to work with more diverse populations or to address state or national issues.

Disadvantages to Working in a Coalition

Coalitions take time and energy. They absorb staff resources and can limit an organization's ability to be creative and independent. Organization periodically must reflect on existing coalition partners to determine whether they are truly worth the time and energy required. Review the next list and then complete the coalition assessment form.

- *Takes time and energy.* Building consensus and keeping people committed to the mission and message of the coalition requires leadership and commitment.
- *Distracts from other work.* If the coalition issue is not the organization's main agenda item, it can divert time and resources that should be focused on other priorities.
- *Weak members cannot deliver.* Organizations providing leadership and resources may get impatient with partners because of their inexperience and inability to deliver on commitment.
- *Too many compromises.* To keep the coalition together, it is often necessary to play to the least common denominator, especially on tactics.
- *Inequity of power.* The range of experience, resources, and power can create internal problems. "One Group—One Vote" does not work for groups with wide ranges of power and resources.

- *Individual organizations may not get the credit.* If all the activities are done in the name of the coalition, groups that contribute a lot often feel that they do not get enough credit.
- *Dull or conventional tactics.* Groups that like more confrontational, highly visible tactics may feel that the more subdued tactics of a coalition are not exciting enough to activate their members.

Each coalition partner will bring a unique mission, goals, objectives, community identity, organizational culture, and public identity to the mix. In assessing the nonprofit's current coalition and partnership base, remember that each coalition is only as strong as its weakest link. Each coalition member brings all of its strengths and weaknesses to the work that the organization shares. It is important to consider what each group will bring to the work: what unique credibility, resources, messages, and relationships that are essential to the work to be done. Consider the potential of the coalition itself and of each coalition member.

Guiding Questions

- Does the organization work effectively with its coalition partners?
- Does the staff use the board to full advantage when implementing its outreach strategies?
- Is our organization working with the right coalition partners?
- Are there groups that are detracting from our ability to achieve our mission? Are there groups that could supplement our efforts if we asked them to partner with us?
- Is our organization currently working with all the organizations that support our mission and our programs?

Coalition Assessment Form

Coalition	Staff Assigned	Time Involved	Recent Accomplishments	Keep Y/N

Creating New Coalitions and Partnerships

Outreach to New Audiences

As the communications action team (CAT) considers the targeted audiences needed to support the work of the organization, it may decide that there are categories of groups or individuals that need to be added to its outreach priorities. In exploring this question, the CAT should ask: Whom do we need to succeed? Are groups that ought to be included routinely in the work conspicuous by their absence? Are some groups underrepresented?

As it targets these new audiences, the CAT must make sure that it understands who they are, what potential they bring to the strategic goals, and what they might be willing to bring to the work. Among the questions that the organization should consider:

- Why are they important to our organization?
- Why should our organization be important to them?
- Where do they get information? Who has credibility with them?

When considering these new audiences, it is important to assess how involved they are likely to be and what it will take to get them to act on behalf of the issue or campaign. The more closely connected an audience feels to a situation, problem, or issue, the more active it will be in seeking out information and acting on that information.

Forming New Partnerships and Coalitions

As the CAT considers the new priorities of the organization's strategic communications plan, it may be important to launch new partnerships to support the outreach strategies.

Guiding Questions

- What is the current relationship between our organization and the potential partner?
- What does the new partner bring to the work of our coalition and the mission of our organization?
- Does the organization have a reputation for working effectively with its coalition partners?
- Are there groups that could supplement our efforts if we asked them to partner with us?
- Is our organization currently working with all the organizations that support our mission and our programs?

Forming New Partnerships

1. Whom do we need to succeed?

2. Why are they important to our organization?

3. Why should our organization be important to them?

4. What do we need them to do if we are to achieve our mission?

Before launching a coalition, the organization should consider each of these questions from both the potential partnering organization's point of view and in terms of the nonprofit organization's priorities:

Guiding Questions

- What are the purposes, roles, and expectations of each coalition member?
- What is the mission of the coalition, and is it consistent with the mission of each potential coalition partner?
- What are the strengths and weaknesses of each coalition partner? How can our organization play to their strengths and rely on other coalition partners to compensate for their weaknesses?
- What do we gain by working with the other members of the coalition? What do they gain by working with us?

Reaching Ethnic Communities

If working with communities with different cultures and ethnic backgrounds is important to the nonprofit, the CAT must consider not only which organizations can help it reach these priority groups. It must also evaluate whether the leadership of that organization effectively connects with these audiences and whether the leadership will be open to partnering.

If the nonprofit is not planning to partner with other organizations, it should carefully consider how well it understands the needs and preferences of the ethnic groups it seeks to serve. Consideration must be given to differences in language, values, historical traditions, and religious beliefs.

Rules of the Road: Building Effective Partnerships and Coalitions

1. Coalition leaders must clearly define the goals, objectives, and tactics that will be used by the coalition. Build consensus around the strategies, messages, and tactics that will be used, including fallback plans.
2. Coalition leaders should appeal to each prospect organization with that organization's needs in mind. Be sure to identify carefully who will win if your position prevails, who will lose, and who will have reasons to stay neutral.
3. For greatest success, coalition leaders need to be aggressive. Identify every organization that should be contacted: groups that will support your position, groups that will be against your position, and groups whose position you don't yet know. Contact each group, and keep a record of their priorities and the facts that influence their positions.
4. The coalition needs to find the activists and put them to work. Do not just sign up the traditional allies of the organization. Find out what each member can bring to the effort.
5. Coalition leaders need to work to develop consensus. Get the coalition to reach decisions and perform tasks. Make the process inclusive; ensure that every individual and every organization has a stake in the success of its work.
6. The coalition needs to learn what the opposition knows. Have an educational strategy of your own and a communications plan to implement it.
7. Coalition success sometimes depends on bringing nontraditional partners together. Establish a dialogue with the other side, whenever possible. Learn their arguments and strive to blunt their criticisms. Try to get some of them to remain neutral or persuade them to join together with the coalition for the common good.

If the organization has never addressed its communications efforts to specific ethnic audiences, it might be valuable to consider these questions:

Guiding Questions

- What does our organization have to offer to each distinct group?
- Are the programs and services that we offer going to be easily understood and supported by each distinct group?
- Are there ways that we can partner together with faith based or community groups to serve the needs of our clients?
- Are we genuinely committed to reaching each of these ethnic groups?
- Have we allocated the resources to provide effective outreach to these groups?

The most effective way to reach a particular ethnic community is to clearly communicate what the organization has to offer and how it relates and can be of benefit to that community.

As part of the outreach plan, it will be important to determine how the nonprofit's leaders are regarded in the ethnic community and by its community leaders. If the organization cannot hire staff to coordinate this portion of its work, working in coalitions and partnership is an effective way of advancing its mission and its work in ethnic communities. Recruiting members of these communities to serve on the CAT or as part of the implementation team will enhance the organization's understanding. It will also give the organization greater credibility as it reaches out to work with them on community issues and concerns in the future.

List of Worksheets

Suggested Resources

Allison, Michael and Jude Kaye. *Strategic Planning for Nonprofit Organizations: A Practical Guide and Workbook, Second Edition.* New York: John Wiley & Sons, 2005.

Bales, Susan Nall and Franklin D. Gilliam, Jr. *Communications for Social Good.* Washington, DC: Foundation Center, 2004.

Bales, Susan Nall and Peg Odel. *Values and Voice: Advancing Philanthropy through Strategic Communications.* Washington, DC: Communications Network and Benton Foundation, 1998.

Berry, Brian. *Strategic Planning Workbook for Nonprofit Organizations.* St. Paul: Amherst H. Wilder Foundation, 1997.

Bonk, Kathy, Henry Griggs, and Emily Tines. *The Jossey-Bass Guide to Strategic Communications for Nonprofits.* San Francisco: Jossey-Bass, 1999.

Bryson, John M. *Strategic Planning for Public and Nonprofit Organizations, Third Edition.* San Francisco: Jossey-Bass, 2004.

Fairhurst, Gail T. and Robert A. Sarr. *The Art of Framing: Managing the Language of Leadership.* San Francisco: Jossey-Bass, 1996.

Fitch, Marc and Patty Oertel. *Getting Your Message Out: A Guide to Public Relations for Nonprofit Organizations, Revised Edition.* Los Angeles: Center for Nonprofit Management, 1997.

Gladwell, Malcolm. *The Tipping Point: How Little Things Can Make a Big Difference* (Boston, New York, and London: Little, Brown & Company, 2002).

Hershey, R. Christine. *Communications Toolkit: A Guide to Navigating Communications for the Nonprofit World.* Santa Monica: Cause Communications, 2005.

Hyatt, Thomas K., Ed. *The Nonprofit Legal Landscape.* Washington, DC: Board Source, 2005.

Iyengar, Shanto. *Is Anyone Responsible: How Television Frames Political Issues.* Chicago: University of Chicago Press, 1991.

Lakoff, George. *Don't Think of An Elephant: Know Your Values and Frame the Debate.* (White River Junction, Vermont: Chelsea Green Publishing, 2004).

McLeish, Barry J. *Successful Marketing Strategies for Nonprofit Organizations.* New York: John Wiley & Sons, 1995.

Moeller, Susan D. *Compassion Fatigue: How the Media Sell Disease, Famine, War and Death.* New York and London: Routledge, 1999.

Patterson, Sally J. *Generating Buzz: Strategic Communications for Nonprofit Boards.* Washington, DC: Board Source, 2006.

Piirto, Rebecca. *Beyond Mind Games: The Marketing Power of Psychographics.* New York: American Demographic Books, 1991.

Stern Gary J. and Elana Center. *Marketing Workbook for Nonprofit Organizations, Volume 1: Develop the Plan, Second Edition.* St. Paul: Amherst H. Wilder Foundation, 2001.

Tannen, Deborah, Ed. *Framing in Discourse.* New York and Oxford: Oxford University Press, 1993.

Templeton, Jane Farley. *The Focus Group: A Strategic Guide to Organizations Conducting and Analyzing the Focus Group Interview.* Burr Ridge: Irwin Professional Publishing, 1994.

Torres, R. T., H. S. Preskill, and M. E. Piontek. *Evaluation Strategies for Communicating and Reporting: Enhancing Learning Organizations.* Thousand Oaks: Sage Publications, 1997.

Weiss, Michael. *The Clustering of America.* New York: Harper and Row, 1988.

Yale, David R. *The Publicity Handbook: How to Maximize Publicity for Products, Services and Organizations.* Lincolnwood: NTC Business Books, 1995.

Yankelovich, Daniel. *Coming to Public Judgment: Making Democracy Work in a Complex World.* Syracuse: Syracuse University Press, 1991.

Index

CPSIA information can be obtained at www.ICGtesting.com
Printed in the USA
BVOW03*0936291214

380847BV00020B/558/P